GW00362100

LONDON'S ROCK ROUTES

JOHN PLATT

FOURTH ESTATE · LONDON

AUTHOR BIOGRAPHY

John Platt is a well-known rock journalist who specialises in articles on the 1960s. He has contributed to many magazines as well as editing his own magazine *Comstock Lode*. He is the author of *Yardbirds*, the definitive biography of the influential sixties band.

He has also worked on several TV documentary series as script consultant and archive film researcher, notably the Channel 4 series 'The Sixties'. He is currently working on a major series entitled 'Rock Family Trees'.

© 1985 John Platt.
First published in Great Britain by Fourth Estate Ltd.,
100 Westbourne Grove, London W2 5RU.
British Library in Cataloguing in Publication Data
Platt, John
London's rock routes.
1. Rock music – England – London – History and criticism
I. Title
784.5'4'009421   ML3534

ISBN 0-947795-70-7

Produced by Charmian Allwright.
Design by Crocodile, London.
Jacket design and illustration by Stuart Jane.

Typeset by Jigsaw Graphics.
Printing and binding by Billings & Sons, Worcester.

FOR ALEXIS KORNER (1928–84) – MUSICIAN,
BROADCASTER AND GENTLEMAN.

CONTENTS

ACKNOWLEDGEMENTS

Special thanks to: Eva Hunte, Richard Wootton.

Thanks to: Alexis and Bobbie Korner, Pete Brown, Mick Eve, Jim Burns, Arthur Chisnall, Alan Synter, Patrick Humphries, Pete Frame, Richard Barnes, Bert Jansch, Anthea Joseph, Brian Knight, Phil Smee, Paul Thoms, Miles and others too numerous to mention.

Photo acknowledgements: BBC Hulton Picture Library – Photo nos. 3, 50; Pete Brown Collection 62; Marc Ellidge 57, 58, 59; GLC Photo Library 61; Eva Hunte 9, 19, 22, 32, 33, 38, 46, 53, 56; Anthea Joseph 20; London Features International 16, 41, 54; Melody Maker 6, 15, 31; Pictorial Press 24, 27, 34, 35, 36, 37, 39, 40, 42, 43, 44, 45, 47, 48; John Pigeon Collection 14, 17, 18; John Platt Collection 8, 10, 12, 13, 21, 23, 26, 30, 60; Rex Features 11, 28, 49, 51, 52, 55; Richmond Public Libraries 7; Topham Picture Library 1, 2, 4, 5, 25, 29.

For nearly 30 years, London has been at the centre of the rock music stage. It didn't acquire that status overnight. But it established a lead, in the 1960s, in a curiously exciting way. This book is a chronicle of that process – and of the clubs, the venues, the bands and the individuals who helped to make it happen.

The background to the story is the city itself and its environs. East, west, south, north: city centre, far-flung suburb. Every part of London had a special contribution to make to the genesis of rock and roll as we know it, from Abbey Road to Richmond, Muswell Hill to the Flamingo. In the chapters that follow, I'll be looking at some of the landmarks of a generation that has itself now passed into history: the 1960s.

But I've tried, too, to set the music of the 1960s in context, to trace a pattern from the postwar trad jazz days and the beat denizens of Soho, through the early enthusiasms for skiffle, soul, blues and rock and roll, to the heady days of Richmond and Kingston and the flowering of the British club scene in the mid-1960s. It hasn't been possible to list all of the many hundreds of clubs (and the thousands of bands), but I hope I've succeeded in choosing some of the more memorable and fascinating venues (and people) of the period.

Perhaps I should add that I've interpreted the concept of 'London' fairly liberally. A glance at the front of the Greater London A–Z street directory will give readers some idea of the territory that I – and that once mighty organisation, the GLC – have covered.

Names of venues that appear in a lighter type can be found under Addresses on page 168 and on the Maps pages 163-8.

SOHO ROOTS, 1950–62
CHAPTER ONE

London's rock routes start in Soho. The 1950s laid the base, carved out the geography of clubs and bars, for the rock phenomenon of the 1960s that this book is all about. We'll be retracing some of the links in a musical chain that stretched through what seemed like a magical era, a decade of rhythm and blues, folk, soul and – above all – rock.

Soho started it – but it didn't happen overnight.

Modern Soho began to take shape towards the end of the nineteenth century, when it was settled by a variety of immigrant groups, especially the Italians. The immigrants, simply by bringing some of the flavour of their native countries to the heart of London – particularly as so many of them opened bars and restaurants – gave Soho a reputation, amongst those who cared for such things, for the exotic and the unusual.

For those who don't know London, a note on Soho's whereabouts. Essentially, it is a square mile dropped into London's West End, bordered by Oxford Street to the north, Regent Street to the west, Coventry Street to the south and Charing Cross Road to the east, although overlapping areas, particularly to the north of Oxford Street, are regarded as honorary parts of Soho.

Soho was an oddity: a village in the city where you could feel part of a genuinely urban life, but live on an essentially human scale. This, coupled with its cosmopolitanism, is what has given it a continuing appeal.

Soho had already become popular with writers and artists in the 1920s. The novels of Evelyn Waugh are full of references to restaurants in the area. By the late 1930s, a genuine literary and artistic bohemia began to develop in the area, centring around people like Julian Maclaren-Ross, Ruthven Todd and Tanbimuttu, most of whom were involved in the resurgence of small press poetry like the Grey Walls Press and the London Magazine; by far the most famous Soho habitué of the time was Dylan Thomas.

Ironically, it was the Second World War that gave the community its greatest impetus. For those on leave from the services it was the ideal refuge, offering a life-style that didn't involve a nine-to-five regularity.

Although the prewar and wartime spirit of Soho continued well into the 1950s, after the war a new bohemian type was emerging, particularly from the art schools of the area. Whereas previously the 'bohemians' had been fairly respectable – at least outwardly – the new generation opted for a good deal less conformity and were altogether more outrageous in their behaviour. To begin with, this new generation were referred to simply as bums, but by the late 1950s they were calling themselves, and being referred to, like their American counterparts, as beatniks or beats.

Two other changes came with the new generation. First, there was a shift from a literary community to a musically-based one. The new denizens of Soho were jazz fanatics, for whom literature, though important, took second place to music. The other change was the unprecedented spread of coffee bars throughout the area. There had been coffee bars (or at least cafés) before the war, but after the first new-style place with an Éspresso machine opened in 1953 (the Moka in Frith Street) the whole area became overrun with them. Most of the coffee bars were just that – a place to go and drink coffee – but many acquired a mystique of their own. Often open practically all night, they became a quasi-secret network

of meeting places for young people, generally run by like-minded individuals.

Many of the beatnik-style coffee bars have passed into legend. The House of Sam Widges, which was on the corner of Berwick Street and D'Arblay Street, was run by Neil Oram, one of the Soho figures of the 1950s and early 1960s. The place had originally been a pub and had an old-fashioned pub frontage painted red. On the ground floor was Sam Widges itself, a straight coffee bar, but one with a great atmosphere, to which everyone gravitated. Downstairs was the music part – known as The Pad – where all-night jazz sessions took place.

Recently Sam Widges has appeared in a work of fiction. Oram's autobiographical, fantasy extravaganza, The Warp, contains a number of references to the place, its clientèle and atmosphere.

Other popular coffee bars included Heaven and Hell in Old Compton Street, which had a ground floor of relative normality

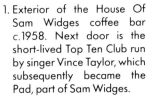

1. Exterior of the House Of Sam Widges coffee bar c.1958. Next door is the short-lived Top Ten Club run by singer Vince Taylor, which subsequently became the Pad, part of Sam Widges.

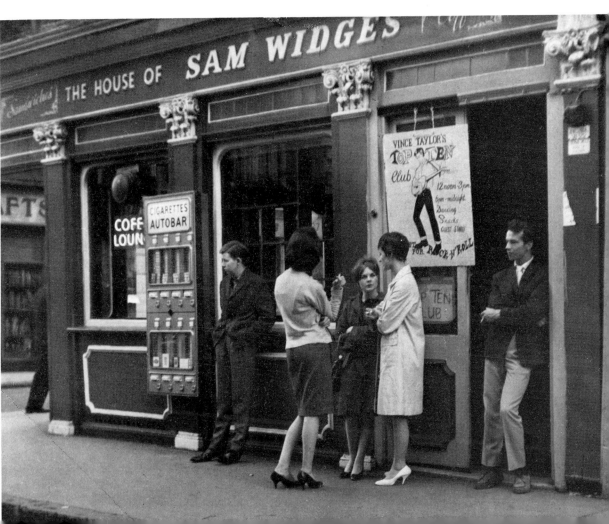

('heaven') and a basement in almost total darkness ('hell'); Le Macabre in Meard Street used coffins as tables and was popular with the Marquee crowd (at least after 1964 when the club moved to Wardour Street, of which more later).

Mention should also be made of the Partisan in Carlisle Street, which was a much plusher affair than most of the other seedy basements. It was architect designed and featured tubular steel chairs and glass tables. Its clientèle was basically the post 1956 new left fraternity, who overlapped, to a degree, with the beat world. The Partisan had a more austere atmosphere than the others – plenty of chess-playing and heavy political exchanges. None the less it was the Partisan which later on (1964) put on the earliest Pete Brown/Mike Horowitz 'New Departures' jazz/poetry experiments.

The coffee bars continued to flourish into the 1960s and were, generally speaking, marvellous refuges, bolt-holes, where one could, for the price of a coffee, indulge in apocalyptic conversation until the dawn rose over Leicester Square.

The coffee bars were, by and large, an adjunct to the main Soho scene, which was, of course, the music: jazz formed the staple diet for most Soho ravers in the 1950s and it was the jazz clubs that formed the first link in the chain that led to the 1960s rock explosion in London.

One of the first was the Club 11, which opened in December 1948 and was run (more or less) by jazz musicians Ronnie Scott (who later founded the famous jazz club that bears his name) and John Dankworth. It was located in Mac's Club at the corner of Windmill Street and Archer Street and by all accounts was a suitably decadent affair, with bare lightbulbs and tatty settees. Being run by musicians, anything went, including something that was almost unknown outside the jazz world – dope. It was dope that closed it down. Early in 1950 it was raided by the police, in the style that became so popular in the 1960s, and several people were charged with possession of marijuana; more surprisingly, Ronnie Scott was busted for cocaine. Later on in the 1950s the premises housed

2. Exterior of the Heaven and Hell coffee bar c.1958; also visible is the 2Is, next door.

3. The Humphrey Lyttleton
   club in the early 1950s.

Cy Laurie's Jazz Club, **at the time the biggest in England. It was there that the concept of 'all-nighters' took off, although the very first all-nighters had been organised by band leader Mick Mulligan and singer George Melly, back in 1951. They had used a basement in Meard Street (at the corner of Dean Street) – premises which have been used over the years for a variety of nefarious purposes. At one time it was a jazz-world drinking club called the Mandrake; for the last few years it has been a rock club. Melly's comment on those first all-nighters is worth repeating: 'Although today the idea of spending a whole night in a crowded airless basement appears extraordinary, it was very exciting then.'**

Other early jazz places included the Feldman Club, located in the basement of 100 Oxford Street, owned by the Feldman family, who included one-time teenage percussion prodigy, Victor. Later (by the mid-1950s) it had become the Humphrey Lyttleton Club, **one of the best jazz venues in London; by the 1960s it had become the** 100 Club **and – like so many of the others – it incorporated other styles of music, notably R n B; in the mid-1970s, it became one of the best, if the most unlikely, of the punk venues.** Studio 51 **was the other early favourite, opening in May 1951 and again located in a basement, this time at 10 Great Newport Street, just out of Soho on the east side of Charing Cross Road. By the mid-1950s it had become the home base for New Orleans purist Ken Colyer and his Band and was known on certain nights of the week as the** Colyer Club.

By the mid-1950s the atmosphere in Soho was electric: the excitement flooded up from the cellar clubs and coffee bars into the streets. Every summer from 1955 through to the end of the decade, a week-long Soho Fair was held, nominally sponsored by the Soho Association to present a healthier image of Soho than the one being projected by the media, who presented it as a place of vice, organised crime and violence – as well as the beats. In fact, the Fair, as Jeff Nuttall puts it in his book, Bomb Culture, **became a 'Festival of the Ravers'. Like**

4. Dancing in the street 1950s style. Frith Street, during the Soho Fair, July 1957.

many other aspects of Soho beat life, its style was dictated largely by the students of St Martin's Art School on the Charing Cross Road. It was they who had decorated many of the coffee bars and it was they who formed the most colourful sections of the parade round the area to the accompaniment of various jazz bands that preceded the fair each year.

The first fair was held between 10 and 16 July 1955, and set the style for the succeeding ones. Taking part that year were such luminaries as George Melly and Cy Laurie's band, as well as various poets. It was like a week-long street party, with people jiving in the middle of Frith Street. It was so good that, according to Nuttall, 'it had to be stopped' – which eventually, after the fourth year, it was. It also provided much of the spirit and the flavour of that other great late 1950s and early 1960s annual event – the Aldermaston March. CND membership was virtually mandatory for all self-respecting Soho beats, and it was they who added the carnival touches to that otherwise rather dour but imposing annual rite.

Obviously, both musicians and audience were interested in having a good time, but many of the musicians also took the history of their music very seriously. A few, notably Chris Barber (one of the most popular band leaders) and his guitar player, Alexis Korner, became interested in an offshoot of jazz – the blues. From about 1950 onwards Barber would break up his gigs with what he called 'skiffle sessions' – a quintet from within the band (including Korner and Lonnie Donegan) would play acoustic but very rhythmic blues, somewhere between older-style Mississippi blues and modern amplified city blues. The 'skiffle' part was something of a misnomer, but the name stuck. It wasn't long before this unit started gigging on their own, at first in a church in Bryanston Street, behind Marble Arch.

Within a couple of years, many of the Soho clubs were featuring their own skiffle groups, notably Richardson's at 44 Gerrard Street, which later became the Good Earth Club.

Totally new clubs opened to accommodate skiffle, the best

being the Skiffle Cellar **at 49 Greek Street, where one of the earliest groups, Russell Quaye's City Ramblers, were resident.**

There was also the Breadbasket, **slightly north of Soho, in Cleveland Street. It was there, in the early 1950s, that Alexis Korner started his career as a (professional) blues singer. Later, in the early months of 1956, the Vipers, featuring Wally Whyton, played their first gigs there. At about this time a split was beginning to emerge in the skiffle world. The more purist element (like Korner) moved off in a more 'genuine' blues direction; others, like the Vipers, opted for a more commercial, white sound. The new sound proved irresistible to the public: Lonnie Donegan had a chart hit with Leadbelly's 'Rock Island Line' as did the Vipers with 'Don't You Rock Me Daddyo'. The audience also split into two: the old audience stuck with the purists; a new audience, mainly the new-style, snappy, Italian-suited teenagers (there on the strength of 'Rock Island Line'), moved in to lap up the more commercial sounds. In April of 1956 two Australian wrestlers, Ray Hunter and Paul Lincoln, took over premises in Old Compton Street (at the Wardour Street end) and opened a coffee bar to attract this new crowd. They called it the** 2Is **(pronounced 'two eyes', and named after the Irani brothers who owned the building).**

In July 1956 the Vipers started playing there; by the end of the year skiffle had become a national craze. The Vipers could feature anything up to eight performers out of a possible pool of around a dozen, including Whyton himself. (Whyton later became a solo folk singer, but he is probably best remembered as the compère of a series of children's TV shows in the early 1960s, notably 5 O'clock Club). **Totally contrary to expectations, the show also featured Alexis Korner's Group, Blues Incorporated, as the regular band! Other members of the Vipers included Tony Meehan on drums and later, in September 1958, when the band tried going electric, Whyton brought in two aspiring musicians, Jet Harris and Hank Marvin. They stayed only a few weeks, however, before joining another group, the Drifters, Cliff Richard's backing band. Within a**

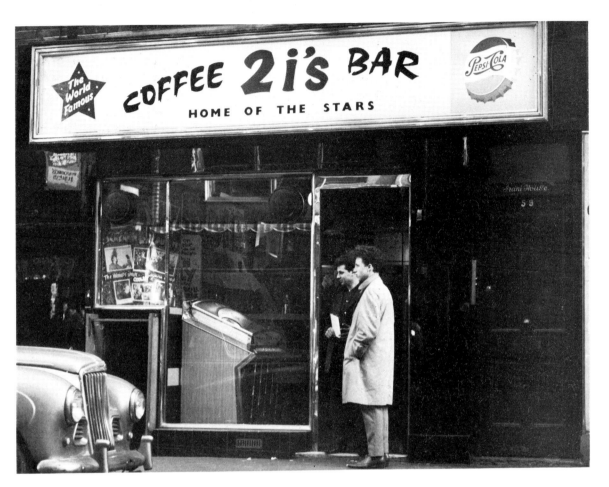

5. The 2Is coffee bar, late 1950s.

year the Drifters had become the Shadows, comprising Marvin and Harris plus Bruce Welch and the Vipers ex-drummer, Tony Meehan. With Marvin and Welch, along with another ex-2Is drummer, Brian Bennett (he'd played with another early rocker, Vince Taylor, in 1958), the Shadows are still with us today, after nearly thirty years in the business.

The autumn of 1958 had been the peak for both skiffle and the 2Is. Whyton says of the place: 'The coffee bar simply couldn't contain the droves of people who wanted to see where it was all happening – after all it was only 30 feet by 10 feet – so Paul [Lincoln] opened a 2Is club around the corner in Gerrard Street.' The skiffle craze had lasted less than two years, but in that time groups had formed all over the country. They had, in most cases, reduced the music to its lowest common denominator, tea chest bass, washboard and guitar – three chords maximum. A few groups were obviously much better than the average and there were a few more skiffle hits, notably a cover version of 'Freight Train' by the Chas McDevitt Group, featuring Nancy Whiskey as lead vocalist. Shortly after the success of this record, McDevitt opened his own place, known as the Freight Train, at the corner of Berwick Street and Noel Street in Soho. Presumably hoping to attract some of the 2Is crowd, he failed, mainly because in London, at least, the boom was over. The 'new crowd' saw skiffle as a kind of primitive rock and roll – and after the emergence of Elvis Presley in 1956, skiffle began to seem somewhat tame. However, it was largely out of the Vipers-style skiffle that English rock and roll emerged, back at the 2Is. To be strictly accurate the first English rock band was Tony Crombie's Rockets, who started playing at Studio 51 in September 1956.

To all intents and purposes the 2Is was the womb of late 1950s British rock and roll, and became world famous as a result. It was the place to be discovered. Tommy Hicks, Harry Webb and Terry Nelhams (better known perhaps as Tommy Steele, Cliff Richard and Adam Faith) all went on to fame and fortune as a result of playing there.

Advertisement for the Freight Train, late 50s.

ALL ABOARD!
CHAS. McDEVITT'S
FREIGHT TRAIN
Junction of Berwick Street and Noel Street.
MUSIC AND COFFEE TILL 3 A.M.

Although many of the 2Is' singers tried hard to emulate Elvis (notably Cliff) and the bands tried to punch out as big a beat as possible, British rock and roll sounded, for the most part, like amplified skiffle, which it was. Most of the artists either went into straight pop and on to showbiz or back to obscurity. Few held on to their roots.

Mention should be made, however, of one of the great showmen of English rock, Screamin' Lord Sutch – who still performs and leads his 'Monster Raving Loony Party' at each general election – plus a handful of musicians like Albert Lee (guitar player in bands backing artists like Emmylou Harris and Eric Clapton) and Ritchie Blackmore (guitarist with Deep Purple and leader of Rainbow) whose musical training began back at the 2Is.

Although able to trade on past glories for several years to come, the 2Is – and the whole style associated with it – had become an anachronism by 1959.

The roots of 1960s rock in London do not lie in the 2Is, however, which was an essentially transitory, if fascinating, aberration. Socially its roots lie, as we have seen, in the anarchic world of trad jazz, with its healthy tolerance of most kinds of behaviour and dress and its fondness for self- – and, occasionally over- – indulgence.

Musically, London's rock roots go back directly to the beginnings of skiffle, before commercialisation set in, and the pioneering work of Cyril Davies. Davies, who was obsessed with Leadbelly, and a friend of his, Bob Watson, who sang Woody Guthrie songs, opened up the first floor of the Roundhouse **pub in Wardour Street (on the corner of Brewer Street) in 1952. It was called the London Skiffle Centre and a number of aspiring artists, like Alexis Korner, played there regularly. By 1955, Davies was bored with the way skiffle was going and approached Korner with the suggestion that the two of them should turn the Skiffle Centre into a real blues club, instead of an ersatz one. Which they did, renaming it the** Blues and Barrelhouse Club, **although most people refer-**

6. The Roundhouse (Soho), late
   1950s. The two guitar players
   are Cyril Davies (left) and
   Alexis Korner, the lady is
   Beryl Bryden.

red to it simply as the Roundhouse. Although it was by no means an instant success, as blues was at this stage very much a minority interest, it later became a mecca, over the years, for both performers and adherents. In the early days, however, performers would often outnumber the audience, but with conversions to a righteous cause being the order of the day, Cyril Davies was heard on more than one occasion to say – with intentional irony – 'You three are very privileged to hear us four.' Even when the club was crowded, half of the audience were likely to be other musicians, who included, even in the early days, people like Long John Baldry, Davy Graham, Brian Knight and Geoff Bradford. All four went on to become influential and respected performers in their respective fields. Baldry played with a variety of R n B groups in the early 1960s until, in an apparent fluke, he had an unexpected number one hit with 'Let the Heartaches Begin' in 1967. Of the remaining three, Graham became the 'father' of the British folk guitar revival and ultimately its most accomplished stylist. Knight and Bradford make another appearance, as we shall see, in the chapter on the Rolling Stones.

It was really the visting Americans who made the club. Genuine American blues musicians had been dropping into Britain since about 1950, usually touring with the jazz bands, but the advent of the Roundhouse gave them somewhere to go and 'blow' on their nights off. Regular visitors to the club included Sonny Terry and Brownie McGhee, Big Bill Broonzy and later Muddy Waters and Otis Spann. There were also a number of white American folk/blues artists, notably Ramblin' Jack Elliot, who was something of a link between Woody Guthrie and Bob Dylan. Apart from his undoubted musical talents, Elliot was the first American anyone had seen who looked like an urban cowboy – tight Levis, cowboy boots, plaid shirt and denim jacket. Single-handedly, he changed the dress sense of most of the Soho denizens who had previously worn long black sweaters and berets (a sort of cross between American beat and French existentialist in style). This new style gradually spread out of Soho, achieving massive popularity in the 1960s; to an extent (New Romantics notwithstanding), it is still with us today.

Almost until the end of the decade, music at the Roundhouse remained totally acoustic; eventually (inspired to a degree by Muddy Waters), Alexis and Cyril felt it was time to move on and brought a 10-watt amplifier — for the two of them! In certain quarters (particularly when they played elsewhere, usually in jazz clubs) this provoked horrified reactions, often resulting in losing the gig.

Ultimately they lost their own gig. In 1960 the landlord at the Roundhouse felt, not that they were diluting the purity of their music, but that they were simply too loud. He replaced them with an accordionist who sang Italian songs — and who was, ironically, much louder.

Over a period of a year or so, the amps got bigger, and drums became a more regular feature, as did a bass (of the stand-up variety). It was becoming rhythm and blues: unlike the watered down version of British rock and roll, British R n B was both exciting and ethnic. Out of this experimental period came England's first real R n B band, Blues Incorporated, fronted by Korner and Davies, the latter having more or less abandoned his brilliant twelve-string guitar-playing, in favour of an amplified harmonica.

More and more though, the increasingly reactionary jazz clubs refused to book the band. The answer was obvious: Davies and Korner had to open another club of their own. This time it was out in Ealing, and it opened on 17 March 1962. This new club, known simply as the Ealing Club, was situated in a basement under a teashop opposite Ealing Broadway underground station. An unlikely venue, but such was the following that Alexis and Cyril had built up that the place was packed from the start.

In keeping with the traditions of the Roundhouse, Alexis and Cyril allowed virtually anybody who felt like it to come up and have a blow. In this way they discovered a whole new genera-

EALING CLUB by A.B.C., Broadway Station, **SHAKE** with the **BLUENOTES.**

Early advertisement for the Ealing Club.

tion of young kids who had been raised on rock and roll, loved its excitement – and were bored to death with trad jazz.

Over the next year or so Mick Jagger, Keith Richard, Eric Clapton and Paul Jones all took to the stage at the Ealing Club, not to mention the actual Blues Incorporated line-up, which included Jack Bruce (later in Cream) and Dick Heckstall-Smith. Ealing proved to be the watershed. Although Blues Incorporated only stayed for about a year, the club had proved that under the right circumstances R n B had everything going for it and was potentially enormously popular. It was from Ealing that it blossomed out. Blues Incorporated moved back into Soho to revitalise the area (as we will see in a later chapter), but with the newly formed Rolling Stones, R n B moved a little further south and west – into Richmond.

STOMPING IN THE THAMES VALLEY
C H A P T E R   T W O

Not surprisingly the centre of London, like all capital cities, was the hub of most of the musical changes in the 1960s. However, even in the 1950s, things were stirring in the suburbs, particularly in the Richmond/Kingston area, some ten miles up the Thames, west of London.

One of the primary factors in this development was the profusion of art colleges in the area, especially the art school in Kingston itself. Richmond in particular was, and remains, an attractive area, full of large Victorian houses, ripe for conversion and without any of the familiar inner-city problems. It may have been more hip to live in Soho or Notting Hill, but it was a good deal more pleasant to live in Richmond – without actually selling your soul to a suburban way of life.

Thus, throughout the late 1950s, the area developed its own bohemian community – although it took a little time before it was recognised as such. The community was scattered – it had no real centre. In theory, 'bohemias' are ideally situated in crumbling corners of old cities, like Greenwich Village in New York or Haight-Ashbury in San Francisco, covering no more than a square mile. On that count, the Thames Valley didn't quite meet the specifications. Like all good bohemias, however, its population required special meeting places, particularly, of course, music venues. One of the first, and probably the most important, was Eel Pie Island, situated on a small island of the same name in the River Thames at Twickenham.

At its best, 'The Island' (regulars never used the Eel Pie prefix) was one of the most imaginative and exciting venues in the country (club – which it certainly was – is far too narrow a description), and in terms of what it set out successfully to do, it was unique.

The name Eel Pie Island was a purely nineteenth-century affair, probably arising from the dubious comestibles of that nature sold at the Island Tavern, later the Eel Pie House and Hotel. Earlier names included Twickenham Ayte, Goose Eyte and Church Ayte. There had been a bowling alley on the island in the seventeenth century.

In 1830 the famous hotel was built, a great rambling affair. The new hotel rapidly became well known, inspiring a deliciously apposite comment in Dickens's Nicholas Nickelby; one of Dickens's characters takes a steamer from Westminster to Eel Pie Island 'to make merry upon a cold collation, bottled beer . . . and to dance to the music of a locomotive band'.

In 1898 the dance hall was added, another splendidly ramshackle affair with lots of arches and columns and mysterious dark corners and best of all – a sprung dance floor.

But by the end of the century the island was past it as a tourist attraction. The island's chief industry became, as it was to remain, boat-building. There was also some residential development, chiefly weather-boarded shacks and bungalows.

During the 1930s occasional dances were held on the island and just after the Second World War a few events such as a 'Grand Jazz Band Ball' took place. In the early 1950s someone acquired a supper licence and music was provided by a tired trio, but by 1956 nothing, musically, was happening on the island at all. It had by then acquired a wonderfully overgrown, decaying and mysterious atmosphere which it retained over the years. But in a few short months the peace was shattered. The person largely responsible for it was a local community relations worker called Arthur Chisnall.

7. Exterior of the Eel Pie Island
Hotel and Dance Hall. Taken
in the late 1950s from the
Surrey Bank of the Thames.

8. Arthur Chisnall who ran the
Island. Taken c.1962.

THAMES HOTEL
Hampton Court, Middlesex
Friday, July 30th
MONTY SUNSHINE'S
JAZZBAND
Saturday, July 31st
COLIN KINGWELL'S
JAZZ BANDITS
Sunday, August 1st
MIKE DANIELS
DELTA JAZZMEN

Early 60s.

BULL'S HEAD
BARNES BRIDGE PRO 5241
JAZZ 7 NIGHTS A WEEK
Plus Sunday Lunchtime
Wed., Fri., Sat., Sun. Lunch & Evening
THE TERRY SHANNON
TRIO
plus
BRITAIN'S FOREMOST FRONTLINERS
Monday, August 2nd
THE JOHNNY SCOTT
QUINTET
featuring
DAVE SNELL ON HARP
Tuesday and Thursday
DICK MORRISSEY
QUARTET
featuring Phil Seaman on drums
plus Guests

Early 60s.

In April 1956 Chisnall obtained permission to use the dance hall, primarily to cater for the art school students and hangers-on in the area. In the beginning, these events were simply free parties with a local trad jazz band, but so popular were they that within a couple of months the Island had become a proper club, booking some of the best bands of the day, notably Ken Colyer's.

Musically, the Island was almost completely trad jazz orientated – double bass, tuba, drums, banjo (of necessity – the guitar and piano in the beginning indicated mainstream jazz) – and a front line of clarinet, trumpet and trombone. From which line-up very few bands in their right minds ever deviated.

Although unique in other ways, the Island, even in its earliest days, wasn't the only jazz club in the area. The Thames Hotel at Hampton Court opened within a week or two of the Island. Kingston also had a number of jazz clubs in the late 1950s. The Fighting Cocks was reckoned the best (it's now the Southern Surplus Store), but there was also the Jazz Cellar and the Jazz Barge. The latter was simply a barge on the Thames owned by one Ian Sheridan, an antique dealer from Kew. The Barge was a nice try, but obviously far too small to be commercially successful.

Richmond itself had the Maddingley Club, housed in a large old house right on the Riverside (technically it's on the Middlesex side and thus in what is known as East Twickenham). Resident there for a number of years was the Keith Smith band, Smith being an early Colyer enthusiast.

By the end of the 1950s fans of modern jazz could go to the Bull (the Bull's Head), down by the river at Barnes. The Bull was for many years the centre of modern jazz in the area, with people like Tubby Hayes (at the time one of the best-known figures in English modern jazz) as regular guests. Actually the Island itself did try modern jazz (or at least mainstream), when Bruce Turner's band played there – but after four months it was decided that the experiment wasn't working. Earlier, the island had also tried Diz Disley's String Quintet, but that too had failed. Disley was in fact something of a local celebrity. A guitarist in the Django Rheinhardt tradition, Disley became reasonably well known in the trad boom days. He lived locally in East Sheen for many years and played regularly at the Derby Arms **on the Upper Richmond Road – a good place, but once again too small to survive. Like the Maddingley, the Derby Arms comes and goes as a club; (ex Fairport Convention guitarist) Richard Thompson played there a few years ago, in its incarnation as a folk club. The Island also ran folk as well, from 1958, much more successfully than their modern jazz experiments. Not surprisingly, folk was very big in the area when it started to boom in the early 1960s.**

The best folk club of all was the Crown **on the Richmond Road in Twickenham. Everyone who was worth seeing on the contemporary folk circuit played there, including Bert Jansch and John Renbourne (later of Pentangle). Later on (**c. **1968) the Crown featured bands during the 'blues boom'. Kingston also had an active folk scene that centred around the** Folk Barge. **What connection this had, if any, with the Jazz Barge, is uncertain – but what is known is that it was run by an alcoholic called Geoff, who eventually became a traffic warden. It was also the place where guitarist John Martyn was discovered. At the end of the 1960s there was an active folk club in Richmond called the** Hanging Lamp, **in the crypt of a church just off Richmond Hill. This again featured all the big names on the folk circuit, plus a few others like the slightly eccentric Ron Geesin, much of whose BBC2 programme** One Man's Week **in 1970 was shot at the Hanging Lamp.**

By far the longest-lasting folk club in the area was (and still is) the Half Moon **on the Lower Richmond Road in Putney. This too was a jazz club early on, but by the early 1960s was presenting folk and later R n B as well.**

The Half Moon is still going, booking excellent acts regularly, and continues to be regarded by musicians and audience alike as one of the best music venues around London. Despite

BLUESCENE. CROWN, TWCK.
STEVE MILLER DELIVERY
PLUS JOHN LEWIS

1968.

HANGING LAMP, St. Elizabeth's
Crypt, The Vineyard, Richmond.
Ragtime.
JOHN JAMES
Recently on " My Kind of Folk."

1970.

9. The Half Moon, Putney, as it
   is today.

10. 'Beatniks' on the dance floor
    at the Island, c.1962.

its (relatively) small size, it still manages to promote gigs featuring big-name artists who work, loosely speaking, in any kind of ethnic field, however amplified and rock-orientated they may be. Thus, in the mid-1980s, people like Taj Mahal, Doctor John, Georgie Fame's band, the Richard Thompson Band and even sixties American rocker Del Shannon have all played there. They also have special events such as the annual three-night Fairport Convention reunion, featuring anything up to fifteen members of the legendary folk/rock group. Folk music remains the core of the Half Moon and so popular is it with musicians that the bar is usually full of performers like Bert Jansch or Ralph ('Streets of London') McTell, taking a night off. Much of the credit for its continued success must go to Johnny Jones, who, although no longer associated with the Half Moon on a full-time basis, built up almost single-handedly both the variety and quality of the acts that play there and helped to create one of the friendliest atmospheres of any London venue.

But back to our rock roots. During the late 1950s and early 1960s, despite the presence of these other venues, the Island continued to be the place to go. Apart from its friendly atmosphere and totally uncommercial outlook, it became a sort of social welfare centre, as much as anything else. It also acquired a bizarre — and largely unjustified — reputation as a centre of all manner of evil goings-on. Virtually every week the local papers carried articles about the Island, usually centring on the supposed drug-taking and wayward morals of the club's members, who were generally described as 'Beatniks'. As a result of the continued bad press, the Island held a benefit night to spotlight the problem, during which various MPs spoke. The matter was subseqently raised in Parliament, and as a result an independent member was elected on to the Press Council for the first time, with the express purpose of investigating harassment of young people by the press. Arthur Chisnall, who ran the Island, commented on the 'truth' behind the allegations about the club's members. 'Our main crime', he said, 'was to get people to think for themselves, an unforgivable sin.'

Despite the occasional foray into other types of music, the Island remained faithful to trad jazz until 1963 and the arrival (on a quasi-commercial level) of R n B.

We have already seen that R n B developed in London at the Roundhouse and later the Ealing Club. Given the nature of its adherents (art school students again) and the relative proximity of Richmond to both Ealing and Soho, it's not surprising that the Richmond area clubs started to shift their musical policy. A notable (and previously undistinguished) Richmond club began life in the back room of the Station Hotel, opposite Richmond station, soon to be known as the Crawdaddy.

The club was run by Giorgio Gomelsky, who was, and remains, a colourful character. A Russian émigré with a Swiss passport, he had ended up in England, after a career in Europe as an experimental film-maker. He was also fervently interested in jazz and blues and became involved with the National Jazz Federation prior to opening the club (in late 1962), after the closure of his Piccadilly Jazz Club, in Great Windmill St.

Resident jazzband at the Piccadilly Club were the Confederates, led by Dave Hunt, who, deciding he no longer liked trad jazz, disbanded the Confederates and formed the Dave Hunt R n B band, which featured future Kink, Ray Davies. It was they who became the first Crawdaddy residents.

When Hunt's band moved on to better things, in early 1963, Gomelsky invited the newly formed Rolling Stones to take their place. As the Stones are a part of a later chapter, suffice to say that within six months the club, by this time known as the Crawdaddy, was bursting at the seams and was forced to move up the road, to the club house of the Richmond Athletic Association.

Shortly after the move, the Stones outgrew the place and once again Gomelsky had to find a replacement. This time a

Advertisement for the Crawdaddy, 1964.

local group virtually fell into his lap: the Yardbirds.

Even more than the Stones, the Yardbirds are woven into the fabric of local legend. Two of them, Paul Samwell-Smith and Jim McCarty, had attended Hampton Grammar School, where they had been part of a school group known as the Country Gentlemen. Of the other original members, two – Chris Dreja and Tony 'Top' Topham – had been at school together in Surbiton and Keith Relf had attended Kingston Art College.

11. The Yardbirds onstage at the Crawdaddy (at the Richmond Athletic Assoc.) late 1963. Paul Samwell-Smith (back to camera) Keith Relf (facing camera): also just visible are drummer Jim McCarty and Eric Clapton.

All had been in various local R n B bands for the previous year or so and by virtue of seeing each other at such exotic venues as the Railway Hotel in Norbiton (near Kingston), had agreed on a merger of the best players. Within weeks of the formation of the Yardbirds in May 1963, they had played Eel Pie Island, Studio 51 in Great Newport Street and were running their own club at the Railway Hotel in Harrow (later a regular Who gig). They were also well aware of the Stones, being regular attenders (but not performers) at the Station Hotel and using the South Western Hotel (opposite the Station Hotel) for rehearsals. It was almost inevitable that they should succeed the Stones at the Crawdaddy.

Initially, they faced the expected cries – 'We want the Stones' – but very quickly they established their own incredibly loyal following. With Gomelsky's sidekick Hamish Grimes standing on a table, whipping them up, the audience would go wild.

By the late summer, Topham had been replaced by another ex-Kingston Art College student, Eric Clapton, who proved to be a brilliantly inventive guitarist. Not surprisingly, the Yardbirds' climb to international fame had begun.

Like many of the clubs, the Crawdaddy was at its height between 1963 and 1966, finally closing in early 1967. The venue itself was used, however, for a series of gigs in the summer of 1968 featuring such bands as Canned Heat, the Nice and Family.

From 1961–5, the grounds of the club were used as the site of the National Jazz Festival (which by 1963 also featured R n B), but by 1966 the festival was forced to move to Windsor and, after a few further changes of location, to Reading, where, with little relation to the old Jazz Festival, it remains.

A number of other R n B venues sprang up locally at the same time as the Crawdaddy. Unsurprisingly some, like the Jazz Cellar in Kingston, had been jazz places before, or continued to run jazz in tandem. One such was the Toby Jug in Tolworth (which later featured Captain Beefheart on his first

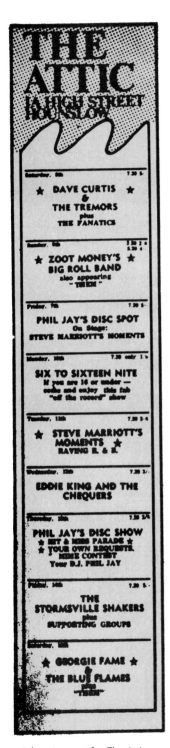

Advertisement for The Attic.

British tour). There was also the Ricky Tick circuit (run by Philip Hayward), the main one at that time being out at Windsor, although later the club moved into Hounslow, a more working-class area, about four miles from Richmond. The premises they took there (opposite the bus garage over a car showroom) had held two previous clubs in the 1960s. Early in the R n B days it had been the Attic, where the Yardbirds, and later the Others (another local R n B band) played. That closed down and in 1965 it became the Zambesi, primarily a black club. The Ricky Tick took over in late 1966, putting on a strange mixture of soul, blues and even the Pink Floyd and Hendrix. The latter were never to the taste of the crowd, who by this time were primarily skinheads. It's interesting that in the R n B days of 1963–4, mods and beats had coexisted to some extent, their common ground being bands like the Yardbirds. Mods never liked real blues and beats didn't go much on pure soul music, but generally they got on at places like the Crawdaddy. Not so a place like the R n B Club in Feltham, again a much more working-class area. The R n B club, known to its followers as Benny's, was located in a hall behind the Playhouse cinema, on the High Street. American soul music was the order of the day. Violence was also a regular feature. Legend has it that a bass player was once worked over for tuning up while a Geno Washington record was still playing.

One of the more interesting but short-lived venues was Tagg's Island at Hampton, on which Fred Karno had built an amazing hotel, resplendent with chandeliers in the ballroom. In the 1920s, the place had been a brothel. According to local rumour, the building was cursed: it was destroyed by fire shortly after the dances began.

Back down the Thames, at Putney, was a mod R n B club, decorated in op-art style, called the Pontiac. In 1965 and 1966 the club featured the usual bands on the circuit, but in August 1965 they put on something special: the Byrds. It was the

Byrds' first visit to the UK, and the public had been led to expect great things, particularly after the massive chart success of their Dylan cover, 'Mr Tambourine Man'. The tour very nearly failed to take place, due to problems with the UK Musicians' Union, but the Byrds were eventually allowed into Britain for a short visit in (fair?) exchange for a visit to the US by the Dave Clark 5.

The Byrds' tour went badly, most reports claiming that the band played poorly and the sound was awful (none of which was helped by the fact that members of the band kept collapsing with flu). The Pontiac gig, by all accounts, was much better. They came on at about 1 a.m., having already played that evening at the Adelphi in Slough, and performed for over an hour, to an enthusiastic audience.

Eel Pie Island had not been particularly slow to catch on to R n B – difficult to avoid it, with the Rolling Stones just down the road – and presented it on Sunday nights. Sunday had featured the Island's only ever resident band, the Riversiders,

12. Unknown R n B band at the Island, late 1962.

It's New ! It Swings ! WHERE ?

Taggs Island

(Hampton Court)

EVERY SATURDAY NITE

Licensed Bars.   8 till Late.   Free Car Park.

TOP GROUPS - DISC SHOW

Free Raffles - Prizes - Mime Contests

Dress Note :- Ladies No Jeans.   Gents No Leather Coats.

Opening 16th July. 5/- with this card

THE PONTIAC CLUB
presents

The Great American Group

THE BYRDS

('Mr. Tambourine Man')

ALL-NIGHTER 8 p.m. - 6 a.m.

SAT. 7th AUGUST

**Plus HERBIE GOINS
& THE NIGHTIMERS**

Plus GROUP SURVIVAL

Plus THE GREATEST SOUNDS ON RECORD!

*N.B. 'The Byrds' are expected to arrive and appear at
the Club sometime between 12.30 and 1 a.m.*

**Pontiac Club Zeeta House
200 Upper Richmond Road Putney
PUTney 2187**

---

club folksville

'half moon' lower richmond rd. putney
every monday

future programme of special guest artistes :

sept. 5 - the ram holder brothers
the well-known gospel and soul group

sept. 12 - long john baldry
the fantastic blues star and poll-
winning singer

sept. 19 - jo-ann kelly & mike cooper
a double bill of two very orginal
blues artistes

sept. 26 - the strawberry hill boys
the famous country music trio back
by popular request

oct.   3 - alexis korner
an evening of great blues in traditional
style by the man who started it all

oct. 10 - the malcolm price trio
the tremendous country star and his
group with their special brand of
music and humour

club folksville's great residents as always.
gerry lockran, royd rivers, cliff aungier, bob lewis

**prices of admission are 4/- for members
and five shillings for non-members**

this has fast become london's top blues and
folk club so drop by and let yourself happen.

13. Forthcoming attractions board
at the Island, 1963.

but by late 1962 they had died a fairly natural death. Amongst the first R n B bands to play at the Island was Cyril Davies' Rhythm & Blues All Stars. Davies played regularly at the Island from then on; his last gig, before his tragically early death from leukemia in January 1962, was at the Island.

The Stones themselves played at the Island about six times in the spring and summer of 1963, and it was for the Stones that a Wednesday night gig was added to the usual Friday, Saturday and Sunday night events. The All Stars and Long John Baldry's Hoochie Coochie Men (the All Stars' successors) were firm favourites at the Island, but just about everybody else played there too. The Crawdaddy, for example, lost a good many of its customers to the Island when Eric Clapton joined John Mayall, whose band the Bluesbreakers played regularly at Eel Pie.

The slightly loopy Downliner Sect (managed, apparently, by band member Don Crane's mother) played there often enough almost to justify describing their appearances as a residency, out of which (along with their other residency at Studio 51) came a Columbia recording contract in 1964. For many people, though, the outstanding player was Jeff Beck. Originally, he was simply a member of the club, but gradually he began jamming with people or playing solo. Eventually, he formed his own band, the Tridents, in 1964, which rapidly became one of the Island favourites. They are mentioned in a song about the Island (called, for some reason, 'Richmond') written by Andy Roberts, who was also an Island regular. Although out-of-town bands like the Animals also played at the Island, the club was primarily interested in promoting groups who had yet to make it, as opposed to already successful ones.

The Island flourished for a further three years, throughout the R n B boom period. By 1967, however, it was obvious that it couldn't go on as before. Chisnall needed at least £200,000 to buy the premises and modernise them. It was too much money. The club folded.

In the autumn of 1969, however, the place reopened as a rock club, with the ludicrous name of Colonel Barefoot's Rock Garden. It was pretty sleazy, even by comparison with the old club – a strictly commercial operation featuring English progressive rock bands for whom 1969 was the big year – Stray, Black Sabbath, the Edgar Broughton Band and others. Half the audience seemed to be police in long-haired wigs. Prospective punters had to walk back past the Bird's Nest Club, where carefree fun-loving skinheads had a habit of throwing people through plate glass windows for the fun of it.

The appalling Colonel Barefoot's notwithstanding, the south-west London suburban music scene had virtually faded away by 1967, a little over ten years since it had come into being with the opening of Eel Pie Island. Almost without exception, places that put on music after that date seemed oddly parochial. In musical terms at least, the thriving local scene had vanished overnight. With a final irony, the Eel Pie Island hotel and dance hall mysteriously burnt down in 1971 – a developer constructed bijoux town houses on the site.

SOHO, 1962–7
CHAPTER THREE

Electric rhythm and blues returned to central London when Alexis Korner's Blues Incorporated moved from the Ealing Club to take up residency at the Marquee. To suggest that they acted as pioneers in the suburbs, building up a following for a year before they moved back to the metropolis, would make for a convenient historical continuity, but it was not, in fact, the case. So popular was the Ealing Club that, by the early summer of 1962, Blues Incorporated were playing to packed houses at the Marquee.

The Marquee had opened back in April 1958, in the basement of the Academy Cinema, in Oxford Street. Prior to the Marquee, the premises had been used as a banqueting suite, but apparently not enough banquets were being held there to justify its continued use for that purpose.

For the first four years of its existence, the Marquee was, of course, solely a jazz club, primarily trad jazz, but with some modern jazz as well. The club's founder, Harold Pendleton, was also a director of the National Jazz Federation, as was bandleader Chris Barber, so it was not surprising that Barber was closely involved with the Marquee at the start. It was Barber (according to some) who had first come up with the idea of skiffle and had done as much as, if not more than, anyone else in popularising blues in Britain.

Like Korner, Barber had been impressed with the electric

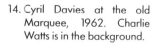

14. Cyril Davies at the old
    Marquee, 1962. Charlie
    Watts is in the background.

sound of Muddy Waters when he toured Britain in 1959, and
attempted something similar at the Marquee, using the singer
Ottilie Paterson. However, his own band couldn't quite cut it
and he brought in Korner and Davies to help out. These
sessions were popular but not entirely successful – Korner and
Davies needed their own band, hence the formation of Blues
Incorporated, who played their first gig at the Marquee in
May 1962, two months after opening the Ealing Club.

   The Marquee remained in Oxford Street until early 1964,
when it moved to new premises, round the corner, at 90
Wardour Street, where it remains to this day. The new club
was actually a warehouse that stood on Crown land, which

necessitated a special dispensation to allow live music and, later, a bar.

The new club opened on 13 March 1964, the bill that night being the Yardbirds (who went on to hold down a Marquee residency and record a live album, 'Five Live Yardbirds', there), Sonny Boy Williamson (who was backed by the Yardbirds) and Long John Baldry and the Hoochie Coochie Men.

The Marquee's policy was always to encourage new bands; this was usually done by offering them an interval spot on a regular basis until they'd built up a sufficient following to headline. This had been the format right from the beginning and was the way that Blues Incorporated finally got R n B a headline slot at the club. Manfred Mann, Spencer Davies, the Who, the Move, Jethro Tull, Yes and more recently the Police, all started by doing the interval spot.

15. Foyer of the new Marquee, 1965.

Over the years just about everybody who was anybody played the Marquee: for a new band it was always a prestige showcase gig. For the record, the biggest crowd ever was for Jimi Hendrix in 1967; possibly the smallest (for a known band) was when only 17 people turned up to see Yes. In fairness, it should be added that there was a blizzard on the night in question.

The fact that the club has outlived all but a handful of its rivals is a testament to the ability of the management to spot new trends and change with the times.

With the success of Blues Incorporated at the Marquee, many of the central London jazz clubs started to move over to R n B.

Partly because of the influence of Korner and Davies, much of early British R n B was rooted either in postwar Chicago R n B (Muddy Waters, Howlin' Wolf, etc.) or Delta-style acoustic blues. All over London – particularly, as we have seen, down in the Thames Valley – newly-formed bands played a Chicago style R n B. A gig at the Marquee was what most strove for, as the club had become the de facto centre of British R n B, but other clubs were nearly as popular – notably the 100 Club. The 100 had gone over to R n B in almost as big a way as the Marquee and drew large crowds, especially when the Pretty Things or the Graham Bond Organisation played there. Generally speaking, postwar Chicago R n B remained the most popular and indeed the most commercial style.

Slightly later in 1964, Korner himself opened another R n B club, Beat City, in partnership with Alex Hermington, located at 79 Oxford Street, W1. It ran during the height of the R n B boom and featured many of the up and coming provincial bands, like the Spencer Davies Group (who featured the then fifteen-year-old Stevie Winwood and his brother Muff), playing their first London date; Tom Jones and the Squires and Them. Them's lead singer, Van Morrison, was notorious for his static performance but apparently at Beat City his manager told him he had to move, so he ran from one side of the stage

16. Alexis Korner's Blues Inc. at
    Beat City, late 1964. Korner
    is nearest the camera.

Advertisement for Alexis Korner's Beat City, 1964.

to the other, shouting his lyrics into the mike as he sprinted past.

Beat City lasted little more than a year, the premises being taken over by Tiles, a much more successful and more commercial venture.

Although Chicago style R n B was the most popular, there was a club at the bottom end of Wardour Street, offering a very different kind of music: the Flamingo.

The origins of the Flamingo are somewhat complex. The original premises were beneath the Mapleton Restaurant at 39 Whitcomb Street, just off Leicester Square. There had been jazz there from the late 1940s, in a club called the Americana, run by Jeff Kruger. In the early 1950s, the club was known, on certain nights, as 'Jazz At The Flamingo'. Also involved in some capacity were the Gunnell brothers, Rik and John; in the late 1950s they moved the Flamingo about 200 yards north to premises at 33–37 Wardour Street. Just to confuse things, the area upstairs was known as the Whiskey A Go Go and after midnight the Flamingo was known as the All Nighter Club.

The Americana had actually been a bebop club and the Flamingo continued the line of development by becoming primarily a modern jazz club.

Modern jazz had always attracted a different audience from trad; much slicker, as befitted the music. By the mid-1950s, the Flamingo had attracted a growing black clientèle, largely American GIs stationed in the UK. It was primarily to cater to their tastes that the music at the Flamingo was, by the end of the decade, shifting towards R n B, not Chicago style, but the modern soul/jazz-influenced variety popularised by Ray Charles and Mose Allison.

One Sunday afternoon in the summer of 1962 the Gunnells introduced the performer who was to become the chief representative of the Flamingo style of R n B – Georgie Fame. Within weeks Fame and his band, the Blue Flames, had become a fixture of the club's notorious all-nighters. Enthusi-

17. Zoot Money's Big Roll Band
outside the Flamingo, 1964.

18. Zoot Money's Big Roll Band onstage at the Flamingo, 1964. Although never achieving the commercial success of some of their contemporaries, the Big Roll Band was one of the most popular London club bands. In the photo Zoot is on the far right, on the far left is guitarist Andy Summers, who many years later found fame with the Police.

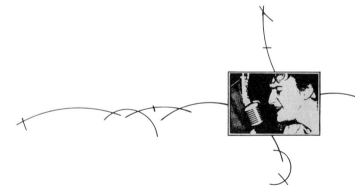

THE SCENE
41 Gt. Windmill Street. W.1
THURSDAY (5th)
    THE ANIMALS
FRIDAY (6th)
TONY SHEVETON AND THE
    SHEVELLES
SATURDAY (7th) ALL NIGHT
    GENE LATTER
    AND THE COUSINS
SUNDAY (8th)
    THE ANIMALS
MONDAY (9th)
    R & B RECORDS WITH
    GUY STEVENS
TUESDAY (10th)
    OFF THE RECORD
    WITH SANDRA
WEDNESDAY (11th)
    BLUE BEAT NIGHT
    WITH SANDRA

Advertisement for the Scene, 1964.

astic members of the audience gave Fame records by obscure American artists like Eddie Jefferson and King Pleasure.

If anything, the Flamingo was hotter and steamier than the Marquee primarily because the audience was a good deal livelier – massive fights being almost an accepted part of the night's entertainment. Around the same time, Fame was also playing in another club about half a mile away, in a then unknown little thoroughfare – Carnaby Street. This was the Roaring Twenties, a long-established club which had changed hands in 1961 and reopened theoretically to provide music for Jewish teenagers. For whatever reason, the expected clientèle didn't materialise, so Fame (who played there) and Count Suckle, the owner of one of the first of the Jamaican-style sound systems, reopened it as a specifically black club. It was at the 'new' Roaring Twenties that bluebeat (the West Indian style that was a precursor of reggae) was heard for the first time in London.

By the beginning of 1963, the Flamingo and to a lesser extent the Roaring Twenties were also frequented by mods, up west for wild weekends that included the mandatory amphetamine-fuelled 'all-nighters' at the Flamingo.

Mods had been around since the very late 1950s, when their style was very much custom-made suits and stiff white-collar shirts. Their musical tastes ran to modern jazz, so that a few were to be found at the Flamingo as early as 1959.

With the spread of the mod movement in 1963, when the style was the more familiar Levis, brogues and parkas (not to mention 'pork-pie' hats, which they'd copied from the West Indians at the Roaring Twenties), specifically mod clubs opened up in Soho. Best known of these was The Scene, off Great Windmill Street, in the old Cy Laurie club premises. DJ at The Scene was Guy Stevens, the owner of probably the best collection of contemporary American black soul and R n B records in the country at the time. Despite the music, or because of it, The Scene was the place for the top mods

('Faces') to hang out and be seen. The Scene also promoted live bands, notably the Who during their High Numbers days, but the groups seemed to have been a secondary consideration.

Despite the popularity of the Flamingo and The Scene, these were still 'early' days (the mod explosion is dealt with in a later chapter) and the predominant Soho style was still art school/beatnik. Musically this meant the Marquee school of R n B (although Blues Incorporated, minus Cyril Davies, moved over to the Flamingo, because their saxophone-dominated sound was more popular there) and folk music, which by the end of 1963 was experiencing a revival.

The story of folk in London in the 1950s and 1960s is a complicated one, partly because it meant different things to different people. In one sense skiffle, particularly the Alexis Korner variety, was folk music; many of the performers at the Roundhouse, like Ramblin' Jack Elliot, were acoustic folkies. There was also a revival of specifically English folk music. One of the earliest manifestations of this (despite the confusing name) was the Ballads and Blues Club, in Rathbone Place, just north of Oxford Street. It opened in 1953 and was run at first by Ewan McColl, one of the fathers of the revival. For several years Ballads and Blues remained a bastion of traditionalism, but eventually broadened its scope to include contemporary material.

Folk, contemporary or otherwise, becomes easier to isolate from the other musical strands with the electrification of R n B. After that point, folk was pretty much any non-amplified music with some sort of ethnic base, even if the lyrics dealt with contemporary issues.

It was, of course, Bob Dylan who gave folk a proverbial kick up the backside, certainly as far as England was concerned — his influence was enormous. Like skiffle before it, folk was something that in theory anybody could play. A guitar was something that you could take with you when you set out for St

Ives, Paris, Istanbul or India. Or even Epping Forest.

One of the first 'contemporary' style clubs was in Earls Court, The Troubadour, which had put on various forms of music (and poetry) for several years. By early 1963 it was almost exclusively a folk club, run by a lady called Anthea Joseph, who has been a leading light in folk circles for nearly 25 years. One memorable evening in 1963 Bob Dylan stepped out of the audience and gave an impromptu performance. Dylan, in fact, already knew about Anthea; before leaving New York Pete Seeger had suggested that he look up Anthea whilst in

19. Exterior of the Troubadour as it is today.

20. Richard Farina at the
    Troubadour, 1965.

England. He was over here because the BBC had asked him to appear in a television play called Madhouse on Castle Street. The play was broadcast on 12 January 1963, but was not well received, although one newspaper (the Daily Mirror) was kind to Dylan: 'Bob Dylan as a hobo guitar player was interesting, although his type of singing could not be judged against this sorry-go-round.'

Whilst here, Dylan stayed in a hotel in South Kensington with fellow American folk singers, Richard Farina and Ric Von Schmidt, with whom he performed in a number of clubs, to a generally poor response. With Farina and Von Schmidt, Dylan recorded several songs in the studio in the basement of the old Dobells folk music shop, 77 Charing Cross Road. His contributions were confined to harmonica and harmonies and because of his contract with Columbia Records, he is credited on the resulting album as 'Blind Boy Grunt'.

A year later Dylan was back, to play the Royal Festival Hall, his only performance except for an appearance (performing) on the BBC current affairs programme, Tonight, a piece of film that miraculously (and unusually) the BBC still have.

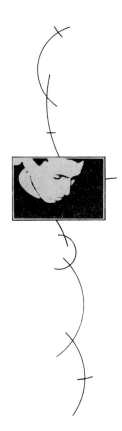

Visiting American folk musicians were common in the 1960s, from the relatively famous (including Tom Paxton, Carolyn Hester, Dave Van Ronk and Phil Ochs) down to the student travellers, who brought their guitars to earn a few extra pounds. Richard Farina, mentioned earlier, was a fairly frequent visitor, usually on his way to Paris or Tangier and often to be found guesting at clubs in town. Farina, a colourful figure who had fought for the IRA in Ireland in the late 1950s and who was a gifted writer and musician, died, sadly, in 1966 in a road accident, returning from a launch party for his novel, Been Down So Long It Looks Like Up To Me, in California. For the last year or so of his life he was married to, and recorded with, Mimi Baez, Joan Baez's sister.

One frequent visitor who later became famous was Paul Simon, who lived in London (sharing a flat with Al Stewart, who himself achieved fame in the 1970s) for the greater part of 1964. He played folk clubs all over the country, as well as that year's Edinburgh Festival and Cambridge Folk Festival. In the summer he was briefly joined by his partner Art Garfunkel. They did no scheduled dates together, but they did manage a brief improvised set one night at a Soho club. Simon's performance that night was watched by a lady called Judith Piepe, who, apart from being an East End social worker, was an important figure on the Soho folk scene, often giving visiting Americans a floor on which to sleep. She was convinced of Simon's talent and persuaded him to return to Britain the following January. Between then and his return she persuaded the BBC to allow Simon an hour in the studio to record some songs for future broadcast. He returned as planned, but the BBC had a problem finding a slot for the songs. Eventually they were broadcast over a two-week period on 'Five To Ten', a midmorning five-minute religious programme. Judith Piepe also interested CBS in an album of Simon's songs, which were recorded on a third visit, in May 1965, at Levy's Studio in Bond Street. The album that resulted was entitled 'The Paul Simon Song Book' and included songs like 'I Am A Rock' and 'Leaves That Are Green', which became a staple of Simon and Garfunkel's set for many years. (Judith Piepe herself — rewarded for her efforts? — appears with Simon on the album cover.) Encouraged by his success, Simon stayed on for another extended visit, during which time he produced an album for another American, the talented, but regrettably largely unknown, Jackson C. Frank. Many people regarded Frank as a major influence on British folk music; his song 'Blues Run The Game', was recorded by various artists, including Bert Jansch and John Renbourne. He is also credited as being the man who taught Sandy Denny (later of Fairport Convention) to play the guitar.

Back in Soho, in 1963, various clubs had already opened or were about to do so, and a whole new generation of excellent musicians was waiting to play, of whom Bert Jansch and John

HIGHGATE VILLAGE, "Gatehouse." PAUL SIMON.

1965.

Renbourne are particularly notable. Although both played regularly at folk clubs all over London, Soho was their home base. Early on Jansch had a residency at a club called the Scot's Hoose in Cambridge Circus, run by Bruce Dunnett, where, even more than the R n B clubs, there were no set rules: Jansch could play for as long as he liked, in whatever condition he happened to be in; he could also invite other guests to join him. A small circuit grew up, comprising the Scot's Hoose Bunjies in Litchfield Street (which, almost miraculously, is still there) and, slightly later, the most famous of them all, Les Cousins in Greek Street.

21. Bert Jansch and John Renbourne on Hampstead Heath, 1965.

Cousins became almost synonymous with English folk. Apart from Jansch and Renbourne, virtually every English folkie who went on to any kind of fame and fortune started there – including Roy Harper, Ralph McTell, John Martyn, Donovan and Al Stewart (who wrote various songs about Soho, including 'Soho, Needless to Say' and 'Old Compton Street Blues').

The club was run, in theory at least, by a Greek with the very English name of Andy Matthews. In fact, the place was run by his parents, who looked after the restaurant upstairs. Wayfaring folk singers could count on being fed by the Matthews, which probably explains why the business eventually went down. Ordinary customers might well have found it disconcerting to share table-space with authentically scruffy folkies.

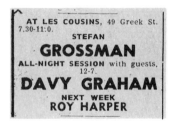

1967.

22. Exterior of Bunjies as it is today. The club was opened in 1954 by Peter Reynolds, who named the club after his cousin's hamster.

THE PENTANGLE
JACQUI McSHEE, BERT JANSCH, TERRY COX, DANNY THOMP-SON, JOHN RENBOURN, THE HORSESHOE, TOTTENHAM COURT ROAD, 7.30 pm. MUS 4832.

1966.

At the weekends, Cousins put on all-nighters — at the time, about the only place in Soho that did, if you excepted the very different atmosphere to be found down at the 'Mingo. As a result, Cousins became an incredible meeting place — for seeing friends, indulging in a little hanky-panky and buying grass. You could do what you liked, as long as you didn't interfere with anyone else — and the music, of course, was usually superb. In a way, it was the social side of Cousins that transferred to the UFO Club at its best, in 1967.

Towards the end of 1966 Jansch and Renbourne opened their own club at the Horseshoes pub in Tottenham Court Road, next to the Dominion cinema. Throughout 1967 they and sundry friends played in various permutations, and they even had a light show — probably the first folk club in the world to do so. By the middle of 1967 a relatively stable group was emerging out of the club, featuring Jansch, Renbourne, Jacqui McShee, Terry Cox and Danny Thompson, who later became Pentangle, for five years one of the most successful British folk groups.

The Horseshoes had opened partly as a rival to Cousins, and musically it worked, but on a social level Cousins remained unchallenged. For many people Cousins was perhaps the last bastion of the old-style freewheeling Soho club, of the sort that had started back in the 1950s.

The other clubs that had that spirit were, even by 1964, losing it. Conversely they were becoming more and more successful. For almost the first time clubs like the Marquee were presenting artists who were commercially as well as artistically successful. The individual clubs were by no means losing their atmosphere — seeing the Yardbirds at the Marquee was as exciting an event as you could wish for — simply that, with the advent of bands as successful 'recording artists', the whole scene became much tighter and some of the old loose-ness was lost; competition inevitably reared its head.

In the end, therefore, it was the Soho folk clubs that pre-served the spirit longest, but by 1967, with folk merging into the 'new' rock (thanks initially to Dylan again) even the folk clubs started to lose their raison d'être.

There was one band who, although they had not risen from the folk clubs, none the less bridged the gap between Cousins and the 'underground' – Fairport Convention, Britain's finest folk-rock band.

The original members of Fairport were all from North London. At the time of their formation, in 1967, Ashley Hutchings (the bass player) and Simon Nichol (rhythm guitar) were living in Fortis Green, near Muswell Hill; Richard Thompson (guitar) lived in Totteridge, another North London suburb; Shawn Frater, the original drummer, was from the same area. Hutchings was Fairport's prime mover, having led the band's previous incarnations (with names like the Ethnic Shuffle Orchestra) from a base at the North Bank Youth Club in Muswell Hill (an early Kinks venue). The band took their name from the large house at the junction of Fortis Green and Fortismere Avenue that had once belonged to the Nichol family, part of which was rented out to Hutchings and used as a rehearsal space. Early Fairport music borrowed heavily from contemporary American sources; from bands like the Lovin' Spoonful, The Youngbloods and The Byrds and artists like Joni Mitchell (practically unknown at the time), Richard Farina and Bob Dylan. What was refreshing about them, even in these early days, was that they always sounded very English.

Frater lasted for one gig, an auspicious debut at St Michael's Church Hall, Golders Green, after which his place was taken by Martin Lamble, from Harrow.

Although instrumentally accomplished (thanks to Thompson's guitar-playing in particular), the band felt the need of a good singer; in short order, they added two. First, Judy Dyble and then the first non-Londoner, Ian Matthews. This line-up found itself playing the London underground clubs, particularly UFO, where they met a young American, Joe Boyd, one of the people running the club. Boyd more or less took over their affairs, booked their gigs and negotiated

23. Richard Thompson (of Fair-
    port Convention) onstage
    at Middle Earth, late 1968.

a record deal. A single and an album, 'Fairport Convention', followed, after which Judy Dyble left, as the band felt that her voice was too light. They carried on without a girl singer, but they'd been dubbed the 'English Jefferson Airplane' (the comparison alluding as much as anything to the presence of a girl singer; Grace Slick in the case of Airplane) and the band bowed to public pressure to find a new girl. They found Sandy Denny, who alone amongst the early Fairporters had 'real' folk music experience. She had a beautiful voice and a whole new input of material, including her own songs, the best of which was 'Who Knows Where The Time Goes', subsequently covered by many people including Judy Collins. With Sandy they were able to draw on genuine English folk roots, which for a time sat happily side by side with the American covers. The next year brought the release of two albums ('What We Did On Our Holidays' and 'Unhalfbricking') and saw the band at its best. The perfect marriage of contemporary folk and rock, unparalleled before or since.

In June 1969 tragedy befell Fairport. Ian Matthews had already left the band when a road accident involving the group's van left Martin Lamble dead and most of the others injured. They continued, enlisting new drummer Dave Mattacks and violinist Dave Swarbrick. But their music also changed; although they remained a rock band (if anything, they became heavier), the American material disappeared and the English folk tradition came to the fore. The subsequent album, 'Liege and Lief', was a landmark – the first truly 'English' folk-rock LP. Shortly after, Ashley Hutchings and Sandy Denny left, the first of myriad changes within the band.

Fairport continued, in various forms, right up until 1977 and indeed continue to reform annually for a festival, held in a little village near Banbury, and a tour – undoubtedly one of the great British institutions.

THE ROLLING STONES' LONDON
CHAPTER FOUR

The Rolling Stones have always been, despite their international travels, a London band. They sound and act like archetypal Londoners and even their music, despite its obvious American roots, sounds as though it bubbles out of the Thames. They could only have come from London.

Their story begins in 1960 when, after a gap of several years, a youthful Mick Jagger renewed his acquaintance with an equally youthful Keith Richard on a train. The meeting turned out to be significant. At the time, both were still living in Dartford, a grey suburban town, about 15 miles south-east of London.

The two had spent their early years together at Wentworth Primary School, in Dartford, but by the time Richard was 11, his family had moved across town, and he had lost contact with his friends, including Jagger. Jagger, always the smart one, had passed his exams and gone on to Dartford Grammar School, whereas Keith, who had presumably failed, went to Dartford Technical College and later to art college in neighbouring Sidcup. At art school Richard was free to indulge his desire to learn the guitar and, with the aid of a few knowledgeable friends, like Dick Taylor, was able to broaden his musical tastes beyond the strict white rock of Elvis into the more esoteric fields of R n B.

Jagger was travelling the same musical route as Richard;

he also knew Taylor, who had attended Dartford Grammar School prior to going to Sidcup Art College. In fact, by the time of the legendary train meeting in 1960, Jagger was already playing in an ad hoc group with Taylor, known as Little Boy Blue and the Blue Boys, but it was all very much on the front room level.

When Jagger and Richard met, Jagger was travelling up to London to the London School of Economics in Houghton St, WC2, where he had just started a degree course in economics. Richard, however, was more interested in the pile of import blues albums that Jagger had with him. Their friendship was resumed and, given the mutual acquaintance of Taylor, Richard was invited to join the Blue Boys.

Things remained in limbo until, in early 1962, they discovered from the Melody Maker that there was a professional blues band playing in London – Blues Incorporated. Despite the fact that Ealing is a good 25 miles across London, they made the trip to the Ealing Club. At first they were totally knocked out by the music, but after their second or third visit began to think that the music, for them, still owed too much to jazz. However, it wasn't long before Jagger was up on stage singing a few numbers with the band. Richard would also play guitar, but his Chuck Berry riffs were felt to be out of place.

By the spring of 1962 Jagger had become a member of Blues Incorporated, along with two other vocalists, Long John Baldry and P. P. Pond (later, as Paul Jones, lead singer with Manfred Mann). By this time Jagger had met Brian Jones, who had come down from Cheltenham at the suggestion of Alexis Korner and was also doing occasional guest spots at the Ealing Club. He, more than any of the others, wanted his own band and consequently placed an ad in Jazz News to find other members. The first reply came from pianist Ian Stewart, who found Jones living in appalling squalor in a flat in Edith Road, Hammersmith. At the time Jones was employed as an assistant at Whiteleys Department Store in Queensway (W2), but as he was fired for stealing, it's not surprising that they never erected a blue plaque in his honour. Jones (who called himself Elmo Lewis at this time) also knew a couple of other musicians from the Ealing Club – namely Geoff Bradford and Brian Knight, guitarist and harmonica player/vocalist respectively, both of whom had been around for some time and had played at the old Roundhouse in Soho back in the 1950s. This line-up, including any drummer that Stewart could find, lasted only a short time before Knight left. He refused – on principle? – to play Chuck Berry numbers.

Bradford left for much the same reason, but only after three new members had been brought in – Jagger, Richard and Taylor (who played bass), plus a semi-regular drummer, Tony Chapman. The group, which still didn't have a name, emerged out of rehearsal sessions held at the Bricklayers' Arms in Broadwick Street, Soho, only about 50 yards from the Roundhouse. Later on they shifted to the Weatherby Arms in the King's Road, as it was closer to the flat that Jagger, Richard and Jones had taken at 102 Edith Grove, Chelsea.

Gigs for the new band were hard to find – in fact, they were nonexistent – until July 1962, when fate dealt them a lucky hand. By this time Blues Inc. were not only playing in Ealing but also had the residency at the Marquee. On 12 July they were due to play on the BBC's Jazz Club radio programme, a night that clashed with the Thursday night residency at the Marquee. At the time there were seven members in the Blues Inc. lineup, and the BBC budget would only stretch to six – Alexis Korner decided to drop Jagger. Although disappointed, Jagger suggested that the Rolling Stones, as they had just become, should fill in at the Marquee; it was their first breakthrough.

They were, however, still dogged with personnel problems. Taylor left to finish his art training at the Royal College of Art (he later formed the Pretty Things) and Tony Chapman, the drummer, who earned his living as a travelling salesman, was away half the time. Various substitutes were tried out, notably Mick Avory, later in the Kinks, but none was right. They wanted Charlie Watts, who had been the drummer in Blues

24. The Stones onstage at their first gig at the old Marquee, July 1962.

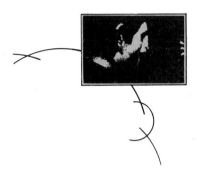

Inc., but had by then more or less joined Brian Knight's Blues By Six (which also included Geoff Bradford); more to the point, Watts was holding down a reasonably successful job as a graphic artist. After sitting in for odd Stones gigs, they finally persuaded Charlie to join in January 1963, by which time they had a regular bass player, Bill Wyman, a veteran of numerous South London rock bands who had been recommended by Chapman – almost the last thing he ever did for the band. Wyman feels that he was hired as much for his superior amplifier as anything else.

Gigs in late 1962 were still hard to come by. A 'difference of opinion' between Keith Richard and Harold Pendleton meant that the Marquee was out of the question for the time being. This left Studio 51 and the odd venue where they could per-suade the management that R n B wasn't an aberration. On this basis they played a few gigs at the Red Lion in Sutton, Sandover Hall off Ormond Road in Richmond and St Mary's Hall in Putney.

CABARET · DANCING

CLUB PANAMA

THEATRE

PICCADILLY
Jazz Club

Jazz Club
ENTRANCE

19ᵉ EDITION

NON
STOP
REVUE

5ᵗʰ WEEK
COME
AND GO
WHEN
YOU
LIKE

CLUB PANAMA'S 19ᵉ EDITION
London's only real
NON-STOP STRIP TEASE REVUE

EDITION

RHYTHM 'N' BLUES
every FRIDAY, 8 p.m. to 11 p.m. at the
PICCADILLY JAZZ CLUB
41 Great Windmill Street, W.1
(opposite Windmill Theatre)
NOV. 23rd
DAVE HUNT'S R & B BAND
with HAMILTON KING
NOV. 30th
RHYTHM 'N' BLUES SPECIAL
7.30 p.m.–12.30 p.m.
ALEXIS KORNER'S
BLUES INCORPORATED
with RON JONES
DAVE HUNT'S R & B BAND
with HAMILTON KING
THE ROLLING STONES
Plus Guests

30 November 1962, the first time Gomelsky saw The Rolling Stones.

They did manage one gig at Giorgio Gomelsky's club, the Piccadilly Jazz Club (see the Kinks' chapter for more on this), but at the time Gomelsky thought they were dreadful. So rapid was their progress in those days that when Gomelsky saw them again, a few weeks later at the Red Lion, he was amazed at how much they'd improved.

At the end of 1962 the Piccadilly Club closed and Gomelsky took over the Station Hotel in Richmond (see Chapter 2), renaming it the Crawdaddy. Brian Jones pestered Gomelsky to let the Stones play at the new club but, with the Dave Hunt Band holding down the residency, it seemed an unlikely prospect. Eventually it was the weather that got them the gig. The winter of 1963 was one of the worst on record: one week the Hunt band couldn't make it and the Stones got their chance.

From an audience of about 50 people at their first Crawdaddy gig, word spread and within weeks the place was packed. Nobody had ever seen anything quite so exciting. All manner of celebrities started dropping in, including George Harrison; media coverage was soon to follow. In order to get something down on tape the band went into the IBC studios in Portland Place and cut half a dozen demos but, good though they were, none of the record companies was interested. All that had changed within two months. The success of the Crawdaddy residency meant that they were able to get regular work, particularly in central London, where they also managed a residency at Studio 51. Suddenly the barriers fell and the clubs that had resisted R n B were clamouring for the Stones and any other R n B bands they could find.

25. Exterior of 41, Great Windmill St (leading to Ham Yard) during the period that Giorgio Gomelsky ran it as the Piccadilly Jazz Club.

26. The Stones onstage at Eel
Pie Island, one of the resi-
dencies they obtained as a
result of their success at the
Crawdaddy (Spring 1963).

Early on in the Stones' Crawdaddy residency, a young man called Andrew Loog Oldham came into their lives. Oldham had always attempted to live a life of fantasy, his early model being Lawrence Harvey in his role of the spiv manager in the early Cliff Richard film Expresso Bongo (1959), wandering into sleazy Soho clubs as though he owned them. Later Oldham amalgamated this with a desire to become the English Phil Spector, the American record producer noted for the unique 'Wall of Sound' he obtained on records and for his eccentric semi-gangster lifestyle. In late 1962 Oldham was briefly employed as a public relations officer for NEMS, Brian Epstein's company, which was his entrée into the pop world. He heard about the Stones and even before meeting them the fantasy of being a pop manager flashed before his eyes. His brilliant sales pitch left the Stones in no doubt and Gomelsky, who'd never signed a contract with the band, was ousted in favour of Oldham.

One of the first examples of Oldham's talents was to negotiate a unique deal for the band with Decca. Apart from a better than average royalty figure, he demanded that instead of using a Decca studio to record (which meant the company owned all the recordings), the Stones would hire their own studio and lease the resulting tracks to Decca. It was a piece of advice that Spector (with whom Oldham had by now become acquainted) had given Oldham, which he'd never forgotten. Decca were amazed. No one in Britain had ever proposed such a deal, but they were so anxious not to lose the band (Dick Rowe, the executive at Decca, had, of course, turned down the Beatles) that they eventually agreed.

The first 'Decca' recordings took place on 10 May at a studio (Olympic Sound, just off Baker Street) hired by Oldham. The initial problem was selecting the best numbers; the Stones' best numbers, all R n B standards, were being performed by so many other bands, and were consequently so well known, that they were unlikely to make the charts. They finally decided on an obscure Chuck Berry number, 'Come On'

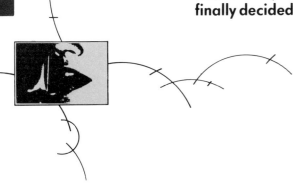

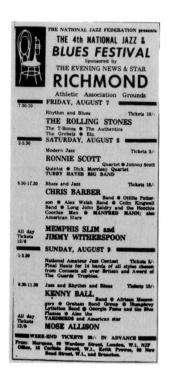

as the A side and Chicago Bluesman Willie Dixon's 'I Want To Be Loved' for the flip side. It was released (after Decca, contrary to Oldham's plan, had been forced to step in and employ a staff producer to remix it) on 7 June. It failed to set the chart alight, but the Stones were now 'Decca Recording Artists'.

With the record doing only tolerably well, they needed an extra push – publicity. Sir Edward Lewis, head of Decca, didn't believe in it, but Oldham thought otherwise. At this point, he came into his own. To start with he cleaned up the band's scruffy image by putting them in houndstooth check jackets. This just about got them an appearance on Thank Your Lucky Stars, the most important pop programme at the time. Even so, their appearance outraged many viewers, who bombarded the programme with complaints.

Oldham's next move was to oust Ian Stewart, the Stones' long-suffering pianist. Oldham claimed that six members were too many on stage, but the move probably had more to do with 'Stew's' altogether sensible appearance and short hair. He was kept on, however, in the capacity of roadie and has always been regarded as the 'sixth Stone', playing piano on most of their albums and frequently on stage during live performances.

The Lucky Stars experience taught Oldham something else – that in the case of the Stones, 'bad press' was as beneficial as 'good press'. For the next 18 months he brilliantly manipulated Fleet Street, planting endless variations on the 'Would You Let Your Daughter Go Out With A Rolling Stone?' theme. The houndstooth jackets did not stay long: there was a lot more mileage in letting the band dress as they wanted, grow their hair and more importantly behave as badly as possible in public.

On 11 August they played at the third National Jazz Festival in Richmond, tucked right down at the bottom of an almost entirely 'jazz' bill. A year later, they headlined a whole evening of R n B at the fourth festival, by then 'The Jazz and Blues

Festival'. It was their last ever appearance in Richmond.

Their first foray into the package tour world started on 29 September 1963, at the New Victoria Theatre in London. Headlining the tour were the Everly Brothers and the Stones' hero, Bo Diddley. Although the tour didn't go too well, and Little Richard had to be flown over halfway through the tour to boost ticket sales, it was significant because the final date at the Hammersmith Odeon (**3 November**) coincided with the release of the Stones' second single, the Lennon and McCartney song 'I Wanna Be Your Man'. The song was given to the Stones after a chance encounter on a London street between Oldham at the two Beatles. It took only a couple of hours at Kingsway Sound Studios, Holborn, to turn the song into a gutsy but very commercial-sounding slice of R n B.

The single was released on 1 November and by 3 November, the Hammersmith audience was only interested in one band — the Stones.

1964 was the really significant year for the Stones. The third single, 'Not Fade Away', became their biggest hit so far. Recorded at Regent Sound at the end of February, the song combined the styles of Buddy Holly (who wrote it) and the shuffling beat of Bo Diddley. The session which produced the song was more like a wild party than anything else and featured, apart from the Stones, Phil Spector, Gene Pitney and a couple of members of the Hollies, including lead singer Allan Clarke. The single was cut at the end of a month-long tour, which the Stones headlined, and which also featured the Ronettes. The next tour, during March, was even more successful, with more screams and, for the first time, near riots.

By this time it was becoming apparent that the Stones were the real voice of Britain's youth. As the Daily Express put it, 'For now the Beatles have registered with all age groups, the Rolling Stones have taken over as the voice of the teens.'

On 18 April the Stones played at the 'Ready Steady Go Rave Mad Mod Ball', at the Empire Pool, Wembley. There were 8,000 screaming fans for the police to deal with and 30 arrests were made. A week later they were back at Wembley again for the NME poll winners' concert, which was preserved on film by ATV and later turned into a forgettable feature film, Big Beat '64.

Stone-mania also reached the BBC. They announced, on 28 May, that they had received over 8,000 postal applications for the 27 June edition of Juke Box Jury on which the Stones were scheduled to appear. Their appearance on this rather staid show was a masterpiece of Oldham-style bad manners; they looked bored, picked their noses, yawned and rarely found anything constructive to say about the records they were supposed to review. The older generation (including the show's compère, David Jacobs) were suitably horrified – the press had a field day and the band sold even more records.

Around this time Oldham realised that unless the band wrote their own songs their success would be limited. They weren't going to get rich rerecording old R n B standards, however exciting they were made to sound. Consequently he

MICK JAGGER   CHARLIE WATTS   BRIAN JONES   KEITH RICHARD

locked Jagger and Richard in the kitchen of the flat the three shared in Willesden and demanded songs. It took a while before they came up with anything remotely suitable for the Stones to use as a single; but at last, in early 1965, they produced 'The Last Time', which went to number one and proved that they no longer had to rely on other people's songs.

Much of the time, of course, was spent on package tours, Londoners only seeing the band on the London dates of a tour, usually at the Astoria, **Finsbury Park (later known as the Rainbow Theatre during the 1970s) or the Tooting Granada. They had played what was to all intents and purposes their last London club date at the end of 1964 at Alexis Korner's Beat City club. It was so packed and steamy that unconscious bodies had to be passed overhead to reach the ambulance men stuck at the back.**

Despite the relative lack of London gigs they were never (thanks to Oldham) out of the press, for 'events' in or around the capital. On 1 July 1965, Bill, Mick and Brian were issued with a summons after an incident at the Francis Service Station in Romford Road, Stratford, East London: in the absence of a public toilet, they had urinated against the garage wall. The three criminals appeared at West Ham magistrates' court on 22 July and were fined £3 each with 15 guineas costs.

Much more serious was the tangled web of drug arrests and subsequent trials that Mick, Keith and Brian were involved in during 1967 and 1968. It began with Jagger and Richard's arrest at the latter's country retreat in West Wittering, Sussex, on 12 February. Marianne Faithfull (later 'Miss X', in the trial) was discovered by the police wearing only a fur rug. On 10 May Brian was arrested at his flat in Courtfield Road (near Gloucester Rd) and on the same day Jagger and Richards were granted £1,000 bail at West Sussex Quarter Sessions. Their trial started on 22 June and they were subsequently found guilty on 29 June. Both then spent the night in jail, Mick at Brixton, Keith at Wormwood Scrubs. Fortunately, however,

27. The Stones looking bored on *Juke Box Jury*, June 1964 (filmed at the BBC Television Theatre, Shepherd's Bush Green, London W12).

28. The Stones during the filming of the ill-fated *Rock and
Roll Circus*, December
1968.

they were both given leave to appeal and were granted bail the following day. On 1 July The Times printed its famous editorial 'Who Breaks a Butterfly Upon A Wheel?' in support of the pair and on 31 July the London Appeal Court quashed Keith's conviction and gave Mick a conditional discharge.

On 30 October Brian was in court again on drugs charges and was sentenced to nine months. He too spent a night in jail, like Richard, in Wormwood Scrubs. His sentence too was subsequently set aside, but he was arrested yet again on 21 May 1968; this time he didn't go to jail.

The pressure of drugs, drink and what he saw as his disintegrating relationship with the other Stones, took their toll on Jones. Just over a year later, on 3 July 1969, he was found dead at the bottom of the swimming pool in the grounds of his Sussex home — apparently he had drowned following an asthma attack.

Jones had in fact already left the group a month previously, his place being taken by ex John Mayall's Bluesbreakers guitarist, Mick Taylor. Taylor arrived just in time to play at the now famous Hyde Park concert, their first, in over two years. Their last London appearance had been the Sunday Night At the London Palladium TV show on 22 January 1967, when they had upset the establishment, yet again, by refusing to take part in the end of show ritual that involved waving goodbye to the audience from the revolving stage.

Between the Palladium and Hyde Park there had been one semi-public performance in London, the filming of the ill-fated and never-to-be-seen Rolling Stones Rock and Roll Circus. It took place over two days, 11 and 12 December 1968, at the old Rediffusion Studios in Wembley, where the last series of Ready Steady Go! had been staged. The circus featured not only the Stones, but also, in various combinations, the Who, Eric Clapton, John Lennon and Marianne Faithfull, not to mention jugglers and acrobats. The film has never been shown in its entirety, as apparently Jagger felt that the Stones (and himself in particular) had been upstaged by the Who. The long lay-off from public performances was for a variety of reasons, notably the effects on the band of the drug busts. Bill Wyman said that this was one of the few periods during which the Stones nearly broke up. 'You didn't know who was going to be in the band from one week to the next – who was going to be in jail and who wasn't.' The 'Satanic Majesties' album, recorded (somehow) during the drug-busts era, had been very badly received, although the 1968 album 'Beggar's Banquet' and the 'Jumping Jack Flash' single had restored the Stones' credibility as recording artists.

The idea of 'free rock concerts in the park' probably stems from the San Francisco, Haight-Ashbury days of 1966, when bands like the Grateful Dead and Big Brother and the Holding Co. regularly gave their services for free in the Golden Gate Park. The idea reached England in the summer of 1968, when Blackhill Enterprises, a management/booking agency who represented various 'underground' artists, put on a series of concerts in Hyde Park, usually in a natural bowl called the Cockpit, alongside the Serpentine. These events, which attracted between 7,000 and 10,000 people (which seemed an enormous number at the time) featured artists like the Pink Floyd, Jethro Tull, Mighty Baby, Fleetwood Mac, Fairport Convention and many others.

Spurred with the success of the 1968 concerts, it was decided to hold more the following summer. This time, they would be bigger and better.

In April 1969, it had been announced that a new 'super-group' had formed featuring, amongst others, Eric Clapton and Ginger Baker from Cream and Stevie Winwood from Traffic – to be called Blind Faith. The first Hyde Park free concert that summer was to be Blind Faith's debut. If the crowd had appeared large at the 1968 concerts, it was nothing compared with Blind Faith's audience on 9 June – an estimated 150,000 turned out to see the band. Backstage that day was Mick Jagger – overwhelmed by the size of the event and the good-natured crowd. The thing was, he wondered,

29. The infamous launch party for the Beggar's Banquet album, held in the Elizabethan Rooms, Gore Hotel, Queen's Gate in London, 5 December 1968.

could the Stones pull a bigger crowd? That afternoon he talked to representatives of Blackhill and, yes, it could be done. A date, 5 July, was fixed. The organisers had less than a month to prepare for this potentially monster event.

The initial idea was a simple 'free' concert, with the secondary purpose of introducing the Stones' new guitarist. Even then they had no desire to exclude Brian Jones; he was

30. Blind Faith onstage during their free concert in Hyde Park, June 1969. Left to right — Ric Grech, Ginger Baker, Eric Clapton and Stevie Winwood.

approached to play. Events, of course, overtook them and the Hyde Park gig became a memorial for Brian.

Depending on which accounts you read, the crowd was anything up to half a million. Whatever it was, it was certainly almost double the Blind Faith figure. Six Granada TV crews covered the day, starting a little after dawn when the overnight sleepers slowly arose from sleeping bags.

31. The Stones onstage, Hyde
    Park, June 1969.

By late morning the music had started. For some bands, like Screw, this was to be their biggest success, and their sole moment of glory, before returning to obscurity. Others, like King Crimson, moved on to bigger and better things. As a mark of respect and an acknowledgement of the past, Alexis Korner's latest band, New Church (featuring his daughter Sappho) also appeared.

The Stones came on at three in the afternoon, Mick resplendent in a white frock over bell bottoms. He demanded silence, got it, and proceeded to read part of Shelley's 'Adonais', in honour of Brian, after which thousands of white butterflies (or those that were still alive) were released into the crowd and the band launched into 'Honky Tonk Woman'. A little over an hour later it was all over; the Stones were back. The Stones, ultimately, were almost a side-issue – they played rather badly, thousands couldn't see them at all and many people on the periphery were harassed all day by groups of marauding skinheads. To have been there, that was the thing; veterans of the day are entitled to refer to it in the same way as their fathers might have talked about their experiences of Dunkirk.

For the Stones it was the end of one era and the start of another. In some ways the Stones have always been the Stones, but that day they left Dartford and the Crawdaddy behind them for good. They were no longer an R n B band, or a teenage girls' band, they were of the new school – a rock band pure and simple. Precocious as ever, the Stones had entered the 1970s in the summer of 1969. It was fitting that it happened in London.

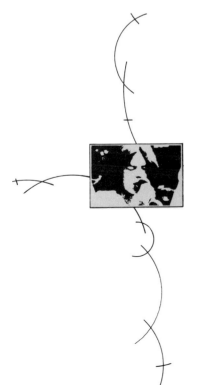

THE BEATLES' LONDON
C H A P T E R   F I V E

It would be unwise to claim that the Beatles were anything other than a Liverpool group. Everything about them oozed Scouse; they were the epitome of Merseybeat. After the advent of the Beatles it was possible to succeed not simply in spite of a regional accent (not just Liverpudlian) but because of it. For the whole of 1963, and most of 1964, Liverpool, with the Beatles at the helm, became the centre of the universe.

That at least was the image – and to an extent the reality measured up to it, except that however nostalgic and grateful the Beatles felt towards their home town, there came a point when the pull of the 'smoke' became too great. They settled for the cosmopolitan delights of London; Liverpool became the place they had come from. Exactly when that occurred is a moot point, but even from the beginning the Beatles knew that they had to deal with London on a certain level. Brian Epstein certainly knew it. As a pioneer, as it were, of regionalism, he knew he would have to take the band to London to further their careers. London would not come to him.

This was particularly true for recording; you could play live all over the north-west, but you had to go to London to record. So it was that the Beatles' first brush with London came with their audition for Decca, New Year's Day 1962. The band drove down the previous day through snow blizzards and stayed overnight at the Royal Hotel, off Russell Square.

Next morning they arrived at the Decca Studios **in 165 Broadhurst Gardens, NW6, and laid down fifteen tracks, all non-originals, as per Epstein's instructions. Considering how nervous they were (McCartney had all but lost his voice), the session turned out reasonably well, except for one small point – Decca were unimpressed and turned them down, on the now-famous grounds that 'guitar groups are on the way out'.**

The tapes were also turned down by most of the other record companies, but undaunted, Epstein decided to have another stab and had a couple of songs transferred on to disc. The record found its way to George Martin, a staff producer at Parlophone, part of the EMI group. He was sufficiently impressed to audition them. On 6 June 1962 the Beatles saw the inside of the studio where almost all of their later work was to be recorded: the EMI Studios, **Abbey Road, NW8.**

At the end of July, Martin informed Epstein that Parlophone were willing to sign the band, but without Pete Best. At which point Ringo Starr entered the story, much to the chagrin of Best's many fans on Merseyside. The 'new' band returned to Abbey Road on 11 September and cut their first single, 'Love Me Do'.

Abbey Road is central to the Beatles' legend. After they had become successful they were granted unlimited access to Studio 2, day or night. Many established artists would find their sessions curtailed when it was discovered that the Beatles wanted to record. Abbey Road became their laboratory; in conjunction with George Martin they revolutionised recording techniques, literally inventing methods of obtaining the sounds they required. This was particularly noticeable on 'Rubber Soul', their 1965 album – a quantum leap, not only in that it was conceived as an album (pop albums had tended to be little more than souvenirs for fans) but also in terms of production – the sound of the bass guitar in particular was way ahead of its time.

Of course the Beatles were not the only act to record at Abbey Road, as a glance at the list of hits produced there

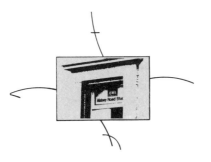

32. The exterior of the EMI
    studios, Abbey Road, as
    they are today.

33. The famous Abbey Road
crossing, taken from the
north, as it is today.

shows: Cliff Richard, the Shadows, Gerry and the Pacemakers, Cilla Black, Manfred Mann, The Hollies – the names go on for ever. For most people, however, Abbey Road is synonymous with the Beatles' album of the same, and the crossing, featured on the cover, is probably the most famous rock landmark in London. The photo, based on loose sketches by Paul, took on great significance for Beatle fans – finding in it all manner of clues pointing unequivally to one fact – that Paul was dead. The album was, chronologically speaking, the Beatles' last. The recording of 'Golden Slumbers' (the last track on the album to be recorded) on 31 July 1969 marked the end of an era.

For the Beatles themselves, at first, London was to remain the place they recorded – for another year, Liverpool was still home. However, Epstein, obviously aware of what was going to happen, opened his first London office in Monmouth Street in May 1963, where Tony Barrow tried desperately to get the band national news coverage. Oddly enough, one of the few news stories from around that time commented on their massive popularity in Liverpool but wondered how long it would be before they left the city.

In April 1963 they performed their first major concert in London, at the Royal Albert Hall, Kensington Gore, SW7 – oddly, the only time they ever played there. It was actually a live radio broadcast for the old Light Programme of the BBC, entitled 'Sounds '63'. The Beatles were well down on a bill that included Del Shannon and Shane Fenton.

In terms of chart success the band had already made it, but it wasn't until the night of 13 October that they became front-page news on every national paper. That was the night they topped the bill on Sunday Night At The London Palladium. It had been news all day, with a growing number of camera crews turning up at 8 Argyll Street, W1 (where the Palladium is situated) to check out the story that thousands of fans were besieging the place. When the show went out it was watched by at least 15,000,000 people.

That night was seen by many as the start of 'Beatlemania', although others argue that it was two weeks later, when the band arrived back from a tour of Sweden to be greeted at Heathrow Airport by thousands of fans. The band had been aware of fans outside stage-doors ever since the Cavern days, but this was something new. It was a scene that would become familiar over the next three years.

On 4 November they took part in the Royal Variety Performance, a more select gathering, in theory, than any they had previously encountered. The show itself was not (as is generally the case) particularly wonderful, and even the Beatles suffered from 'Royal flu' to an extent. However, when the TV recording was broadcast the following week, 26,000,000 watched it.

As a Christmas special they put on a short tour, along with other Epstein artists, that, although it stopped off in Liverpool, significantly finished in London at the Finsbury Park Astoria. The Christmas show the following year was held at the Hammersmith Odeon (and featured, amongst other things, the Beatles in Dr Who 'Yeti' outfits).

By early 1964 the Beatles had all settled in London. Paul had already moved into a flat in the home of actress Jane Asher's family at 57 Wimpole Street. He lived there until 1966, when he bought a house in Cavendish Avenue, NW8. John and Cynthia

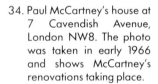

34. Paul McCartney's house at 7 Cavendish Avenue, London NW8. The photo was taken in early 1966 and shows McCartney's renovations taking place.

35. The Beatles onstage at the
    Wimbledon Palais, 14
    December 1963, as part of
    the 'Southern Area Fan
    Club Convention'.

moved into their first London flat, in Emperor's Gate, SW7 (near the Albert Hall) in early 1964, but stayed only a few months before moving out to Weybridge. Ringo and George shared a flat in William Mews, Knightsbridge, but after a burglary in April 1964 went their separate ways.

Although they were all living in London, the most significant split with their home town came after the Liverpool première of their first film, A Hard Day's Night, in July 1964. After the première they were cheered by 50,000 fans, but flew straight back to London, for the London première at the London Pavilion, in Piccadilly W1. Their hasty departure did not go unremarked in Merseyside.

For another two years, Beatlemania continued to boom. They were touring constantly, and rarely playing in London, let alone Liverpool. But for Londoners there was always the Christmas show or the annual NME award winners' concert at Wembley (the Beatles played each year from 1964–6). Eventually even the touring stopped; the band played its last concert in England at the NME concert at Wembley on 1 May 1966 and the last one ever in San Francisco, on 29 August 1966. That was not, of course, the end of the Beatles. Beatlemania might have waned, but anything they did or said was still very big news. Every change in their appearance (particularly during the beads and flower era) was minutely examined as were, of course, their music and films. All the Beatle films have some London locations, notably out at Twickenham (Hard Day's Night and Help! were partly shot at Twickenham Studios). In Help!, a whole street (Ailsa Avenue, not far from the studios) was turned into a set. Magical Mystery Tour, although shot mainly in Devon, has a scene in Raymond's Revuebar Theatre, a well-known strip club in Walker Court, Soho.

When the touring stopped the Beatles looked around for something to do with their money – and came up with Apple. The first public manifestation of Apple was the launching of the Apple Boutique at 94 Baker Street on 5 December 1967, a building they'd had adorned with a giant mural designed by a

36. Première of the *Hard Day's Night* film, at the London Pavillion, July 1964.

group of Dutch artists and designers known as 'The Fool'. The mural was eventually removed because of protests from local residents; and shortly after, the business went down the tube on 30 July 1968. As a final gesture the remaining £13,000 worth of stock was given away.

Earlier, in May 1968, Lennon and McCartney had announced the various aspects of the Apple empire, which apart from the boutique was to include Apple Records and Apple Films. After a brief stay at offices at 95 Wigmore Street, the organisation moved to luxurious offices at 3 Savile Row. The only side of the business that was a success was, not surprisingly, Apple Records, since they continued to release the Beatles records, and then, after the split, the solo records. In 1972 the whole operation began to fall apart at the seams, amidst a flood of law suits. There is still an Apple office today, at 29 St James's Street, but with the individual Bealts' affairs handled by their own offices, it bears little relation to the once great enterprise. For many people, the fondest memory of the whole era was a brief concert the band gave from the roof of Savile Row, included in the film Let It Be. That concert, 30 January 1969, ends with John saying, 'Did we pass the audition?' They had come full-circle from New Year's Day 1962, their first 'appearance' in London, when they had failed a very different audition.

37. Exterior of the Apple office
    at 3 Savile Row, in early
    1969.

WEST MEETS EAST – THE LONDON OF THE WHO AND THE SMALL FACES

CHAPTER SIX

The Who, more than any other band mentioned in this book, were a London band, or, to be more exact, the archetypal West London band. They all came more or less from the same area and unlike, say, the Stones, their early successes were within that area.

The story starts around 1962 in the West London suburb of Acton, a predominantly, but not exclusively, working-class district about 10 miles from the city. Amongst the pupils at the local grammar school were Pete Townshend and John Entwistle, who, when they were about 14, formed a trad jazz group called the Confederates. The Confederates never really played publicly except at the Acton Congo Club, a youth club attached to the Congregational Church. Members came and went and the band evolved into two further groups, the Aristocrats and then the Scorpions, by which time the jazz had all but been replaced by Shadows-style instrumentals. Shortly after the formation of the Scorpions, Entwistle ran into Roger Daltrey, who had also been at Acton Grammar but had left the previous year. As a result of the meeting Entwistle joined Daltrey's band the Detours, who actually played gigs and made money. Not long after, Townshend joined as well, although at the time, and for some while after, he played rhythm guitar, Daltrey played lead and they had a different lead singer (who was later ousted).

Initially they played one-off gigs, usually local firms' dances, but they did do an unlikely series of gigs in South London at a club called the Paradise in Peckham. However, at the time, the height of most groups' ambitions was to break into the suburban ballroom circuit. Each area of London had one, usually controlled by one promoter, and they were a million miles away from the bohemian decadence of the Soho jazz clubs or Eel Pie Island.

The local circuit was operated by Bob Druce and at some point during late 1962 the Detours auditioned for him, in front of an audience at the Oldfield Hotel in Greenford, slightly north and west of Acton – they passed. Apart from sending them with bizarre regularity to a gig in Broadstairs, on the Kent coast, they also played all the major venues on Druce's circuit n North and West London, primarily the White Hart Hotel at 264 Acton High Street, the Fox and Goose in Hanger Lane, Ealing, the White Hart in Southall and the Goldhawk Social Club, Goldhawk Road, Shepherd's Bush. They also did the occasional 'prestige' gig at somewhere like Acton Town Hall.

Around this time Townshend started to attend Ealing Art College, in St Mary's Road, Ealing, just down the road from where he had grown up, near Ealing Common. While there Pete discovered various things that were to have a bearing on his work with the Who: autodestructive art, dope and – via an American student's record collection – R n B. Townshend was to spend many hours in the American's flat in Sunnyside Road, opposite the college, endlessly playing the records, which he eventually inherited. It was not long before a few R n B numbers began creeping into the Detours' set, which was already moving away from Cliff and the Shadows material as a result of seeing Johnny Kidd and the Pirates. The gig with Kidd (one of the few genuine English rockers still playing at that time) was one of a number that the Detours played for Druce, supporting currently well-known artists like Shane Fenton and Brian Poole and the Tremeloes. Usually these took

38. Front entrance of the Goldhawk Social Club, an early Who stronghold, as it is today.

place out of the area, at two of Druce's other locations, the Glenlyn Ballroom in Forest Hill and St Mary's Ballroom in Putney. It was at St Mary's that they first played with the Stones, who were just starting to make a name for themselves.

In early 1964, the Who discovered the existence of another band called the 'Detours' and consequently had to change their name; after the statutory period of deliberation, they became the Who.

Shortly after adopting the new name, they obtained a residency at the Railway Hotel in Harrow, a club run by Richard Barnes, who was at college with Townshend. The Railway had been putting on R n B and related music for about 18 months; Cyril Davies had opened it up as a venue and the previous summer the Yardbirds had run their own club there. Slowly but surely the band was building up a solid following and in a few places had pockets of hardcore fans, notably at the Goldhawk Club, the Trade Union Hall in Watford, the Assembly Rooms, Carpenters Park and, before long, at the Railway as well. It was at the Railway that Townshend started smashing guitars: the archetypal Who trademark.

It was inevitable that they would have to break out of the Druce circuit and two things happened in early 1964 to accelerate the move to bigger things. First, they decided they needed a new drummer and acquired the services of Keith Moon who, at the time, was playing in another Druce band, the Beachcombers. Moon was not only a better drummer than their existing one, Dougie Sandom, but was also very flash, giving a much needed boost to their image. They received an even bigger boost when they became involved with Pete Meaden, an incredibly intense man who had worked with Andrew Oldham, handling the Stones' publicity. Meaden was a mod; in fact he lived, ate and slept mod and his ambition was to turn the Who into the premier mod band. He decked them out in mod clothes, took them to the Scene club (where they later played) and introduced them to the top mods.

He also got them to record their first single. 'I'm The

Face'/'Zoot Suit,' both reworkings of R n B songs. It was, as Meaden's press release suggested, the first genuine mod single. The record was issued under the band name of the High Numbers, as Meaden had persuaded the band to drop the Who in favour of a more mod name – a 'Number' being a type of mod.

Shortly after the release of the record in July 1964, two young film directors, Kit Lambert and Chris Stamp (brother of actor Terence Stamp) approached the band with the idea of making a film with them, having been attracted by the excitement they generated on stage. In due course the two became the band's managers, despite knowing next to nothing about the pop business. They had all kinds of grandiose schemes, some of which actually worked, although for several years they were always losing money. Part of their major contribution was to encourage Townshend's songwriting. In fact they installed him in the flat above their offices at 84 Eaton Place, Belgravia, to get him away from his art school 'decadence'.

By this time the High Numbers had established themselves as the leading mod band and were playing in the new clubs all around London; however, other than a couple of gigs at the Scene and the 100 Club, they had yet to make an impact in central London. This was rectified by the major coup, towards the end of 1964, of obtaining a residency at the Marquee on Tuesday nights. Just before they started, Lambert changed the name back to the Who, which led to their famous poster (originally for the Marquee gigs), 'The Who – Maximum R&B'.

Success, of a kind, seemed just around the corner. The first two Who singles were well received and the third, 'My Generation', was a smash, becoming a rock anthem. However, with their debts, legal problems and internal feuds the next three years were as much a desperate attempt to hold things together as anything else. Despite the astonishing development of Townshend as a songwriter and the excitement of both their live act and their records, the Who found it hard to move up in the way the Stones had done. They were still

39. The Who onstage at the
Marquee, 1965.

40. The Who discuss a legal
    matter in Hyde Park, 1965.

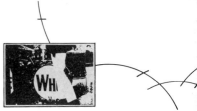

essentially on the club circuit during 1965 and 1966. 1967
proved to be a better year as they began to attract a wider
following in the UK (particularly as they had shed the mod
image), playing at various 'all-night raves' plus a couple of

41. The Who performing 'Tommy' at Ronnie Scott's club, Soho, May 1969.

successful concerts at London's Saville Theatre in Shaftesbury Avenue (notably one with the relatively unknown Jimi Hendrix, on 29 January).

Success came in the US that year, after their appearance at the Monterey Festival in June, and for the next 18 months much of their time was spent in America, to the detriment of their careers in the UK.

In the end, of course, they received their just deserts with 'Tommy', the rock-opera that they had worked on for most of the latter half of 1968. Just before its release in May 1969, the band performed it in its entirety for the press at Ronnie Scott's Jazz Club, in Soho. It was a new invigorated Who. After six years of slogging they had finally made it. From now on the venues they played were places like the Fairfield Hall in Croydon, where they played in September 1969, the first time they had played in the UK without a support band. To promote 'Tommy' they played genuine opera houses, including the London Coliseum. The days of Townshend smashing his guitar into the ceiling of the Railway Hotel had gone, but, like the Stones there was no way to escape the fact that the Who were still a London band.

The Who, as we have seen, were the quintessential West London band – but East London had venues and bands that were as individualistic, and as representative of that side of the capital, as the Who were of the territory to the West.

Back in the late 1950s, in the early days of rock and roll, clubs were almost non-existent, certainly outside of Soho. Promoters, with an eye to the main chance, would hire a hall, book a couple of bands, stick up the posters and hope for the best. Most of these early entrepreneurs went back to selling used cars, but a few succeeded, building little empires on the way.

One such was Ron King who – in partnership with a barber from Stamford Hill called Alex – had the whole of North-east and East London 'sewn up' by 1959. King was a colourful character, with guard dogs and 'heavies', neither of which were probably necessary to protect the average £200 door take, of which the band would get £15 to £20. King booked such exotic venues as the Wykeham Hall, Romford, situated in the Market Square, a very big Saturday night gig; the Waltham Cross Drill Hall (a place so depressing that fights were the only way for the punters to keep their spirits up); the Royal Forest Hotel, Chingford; the East Ham Liberal Club plus a number of other town halls, baths and the like.

The bands King booked were essentially first-generation rockers like Rory Blackwell and manager Larry Parnes' stable (Duffy Power, Marty Wilde, Dickie Pride, etc). Although most of these early rockers tend to be dismissed, some were actually very good, notably Pride, who was known as the 'Guvnor' not just for his voice but because he was probably the first British rocker to introduce obscure modern American 'soul' material, particularly songs by King Pleasure.

With the 1960s, of course, came the club boom, but oddly, the East End produced very few clubs or venues of any sort throughout the decade. One exception was the Upper Cut Club, located on Woodgrange Road, Forest Gate. The Upper Cut, which ran throughout the late 1960s, was owned by heavyweight boxer, Billy Walker. Although various rock and blues acts played there, the Upper Cut was a more soul-orientated affair and conceived on a rather grand scale. You could even buy tickets in advance by post and their press adverts were usually three times the size of most other clubs'. (The Upper Cut was not, in fact, Walker's first venture into music. In 1964 he'd recorded a single, 'A Certain Girl', a song which was also, coincidentally, the B side of the first Yardbirds single.)

Apart from the Upper Cut, almost the only other venue was the East Ham Granada, a perennial staging post on those endless 1960s package tours. During the blues boom of 1968–9, a few small-time clubs did appear, notably the Bottleneck Blues Club in Angel Lane, E15. If there were few

BOTTLENECK BLUES CLUB
BOND ST. BLUES
Pale Green Limousine Lights
Railway Tavern, Angel Lane,
Stratford, E.15. Don't forget
Match of the Day Johns.

1968.

FRIDAY, 10th NOVEMBER
RAVE—
RAVE—
RAVE—
LEN MARSHALL SHOW
Top Groups — Light Show
7.30-11.00

THE UPPER CUT
WOODGRANGE ROAD
FOREST GATE, E.7

Saturday Afternoon November 11th
GIGGLE GOGGLE GUGGLE
Prizes   Groups
Mike Quinn
2.30-5.00   2/6

SATURDAY, 11th NOVEMBER, 7.30-11.45

★ **JOHN MAYALL** ★
and RAVE BOUTIQUE FASHION SHOW
Golden Door Competition   GO-GO GIRLS

SUNDAY, 12th NOVEMBER, 4 SEMI-FINALISTS

DISCOVERIES OF TOMORROW BEAT CONTEST
£1,000 in Prizes. First Prize £500 voucher for
MARSHALL EQUIPMENT

SEMI-FINALISTS: **JOHNNY & THE RIVALS**   •   **SYRIAN BLUES**
SOUNDS LIKE SIX   •   **BOHEMIANS**

BREAKTHRU • D. J. CHRIS WINDSOR

NOVEMBER 18th

EXPLOSION ONE
P. P. ARNOLD
+ FOURMOST
+ MAN EE GO

EXPLOSION TWO
BEN-E-KING
AND THE SENATE

EXPLOSION THREE
EDDIE FLOYD+
SOUNDS INCORPORATED
+
EBONY KEYS

BLAST OFF NOW!!
AND SAVE 9/6

BY BOOKING IN ADVANCE WITH A 3 FOR 1 TICKET

P/O — MONEY ORDER — CHEQUE
I enclose £1 for a 3 for 1 Ticket

P.P. ARNOLD SHOW 9/6 ....
BEN-E-KING SHOW   7/6 ....
EDDIE FLOYD   12/6 ....
ADVANCE   10/– ....

3 POWER-PACKED SHOWS
FOR £1, SAVE 9/6
To: THE UPPER CUT
Woodgrange Road, Forest Gate, E.7

NAME ....
ADDRESS ....
....

The Upper Cut available for private bookings.   Phone 01-534 6578

venues, there was one band of the era inextricably linked with the East End: the Small Faces.

Their story starts in early 1965 in the unlikely surroundings of the J60 Music Bar in East Ham. Working behind the counter was a diminutive ex child actor, Steve Marriott, whose most famous work had been as a telegram boy in a 1963 film about a pop group called Live It Up. Also starring in the film were an equally youthful David Hemmings, and Heinz (Burt) who'd had a couple of hits and was thus the best known of the three. The group (of which all three were members and whose struggle for fame is the film's central plot) become a success in the final reel and their future is assured. After the film Marriott did form a real group, the Moments, who gigged around the London club circuit and released a single but, unlike the group in the film, they went nowhere. Hence the part-time job in the music shop. One Saturday morning another voluble and undersized local lad came in to buy a bass guitar. His name was Ronnie Lane. The two took to each other straight away, discovering a mutual interest in obscure soul music.

Lane was also in a local band, the Outcasts, and one night, soon after their first meeting, Lane invited Marriott down to the British Prince pub in Ilford, to sit in. Steve later said of the evening, 'I turned up complete with harmonica and me and Ronnie started drinking whisky, really knocking them back until we were really pissed. For a finale we treated the audience to a raving Jerry Lee Lewis number which ended with me smashing the piano. We were sacked instantly and banned from the pub.' An auspicious beginning.

The performance that night, not surprisingly, was the band's last — probably no great loss to the world of music. Afterwards, however, Marriott and Lane decided to form a new band. They kept the Outcasts' drummer, Kenny Jones, Ronnie carried on with the bass (which he'd only been playing since the day he met Marriott) and Steve volunteered to learn the guitar. One of the other customers at the J60 was Jimmy Langwith, whose parents ran a pub in East Ham called the

Ruskin Arms. Langwith had an organ, but, more importantly, he had an old van – so he was asked to join.

After the briefest of rehearsal periods they decided to go out and play. For reasons never satisfactorily explained, their first gig was at the Mojo Club in Sheffield, a club owned by Peter Stringfellow, now the owner of a chic night club/wine bar in London which bears his name. Back in the East End they took to playing in the Ruskin Arms; it was there that they were spotted by the owners of a new (and as it turned out fairly short-lived) club called the Cavern – not the famous Liverpudlian original but a namesake, just off Leicester Square, in basement premises next door to the Prince Charles cinema in Leicester Place. For their West End debut they needed a new name (in fact, they don't seem to have had one before) and Steve's girlfriend Annie came up with the Small Faces – on the grounds, presumably, that they were all small (except Langwith) and were all out and out mods. A top mod was known as a Face. Hence, 'Small Faces'.

Unlike the Who, who had their mod image grafted on, the Small Faces were the genuine article. They were to become the **mod group**.

The Cavern gig went so well that it led to a residency. What they lacked in musical ability (and the fact that they only knew about five numbers) they made up for in sheer nerve, although Marriott's voice was already being noted for its unique, soulful quality.

From the Cavern they went on to the club circuit and quite quickly were playing gigs in the Midlands and the North. These out-of-town gigs were strictly one-offs: the band still had day jobs in the East End, although these didn't last long. Ronnie Lane and Kenny Jones both worked for Selmer Amplifiers in their warehouse, but were both sacked for sundry misdemeanours. Later Ronnie worked for the Ministry of Defence, allegedly ferrying plans for nuclear submarines between offices, amongst other things.

By the middle of 1965 the group had gone professional and

obtained proper management, having signed with Don Arden, a well-respected individual with a growing stable of stars. In his office above Carnaby Street, Arden not only offered them a salary but an account at every boutique in the street below. Lane recalled 'We had twenty pounds a week expenses and accounts at every clothes shop . . . we were like a bunch of old women at a jumble sale. Some of the stuff we never even wore.' It was 18 months before they realised it wasn't such a good deal after all.

The summer of 1965 saw the release of their first single 'Watcha Gonna Do About It?', which despite blatantly

42. The Small Faces taking advantage of their account at a Carnaby Street boutique, early 1965.

plagiarising a Soloman Burke song, was good enough to make the Top 20. Shortly afterwards Jimmy Winston (Langwith's stage-name) was fired, to be replaced by Ian MacLagen, previously organist with The Boz People and an altogether better musician.

Although not all their singles of the next year or so were hits, the band themselves became incredibly popular, regularly appearing on TV shows like Thank Your Lucky Stars and Ready Steady Go! They even appeared in an awful feature film called Dateline Diamonds, a weak-kneed thriller involving car chases around central London, in which the band play in a hall in Watford. The film also features several pirate radio DJs and a pirate radio ship.

Gradually their image changed; by the beginning of 1967 the four little mods could be seen to be growing up. The hair was getting longer, the clothes were more sophisticated. And they'd moved away from the East End and were living in a house in Pimlico. Other things were changing as well; at the end of 1966 they left Arden and Decca (their record label) and signed with Immediate, Andrew Loog Oldham's label. Oldham also became their manager and raised their salaries to sixty pounds a week each.

Their music was also changing and the Marriott-Lane songwriting partnership was beginning to blossom. Although still rooted in soul, the pair came up with increasingly sophisticated lyrics and melodies, frequently borrowing on their past. 'Here Comes The Night' is about the early pill-popping mod days and 'Itchycoo Park' is reputed to be a piece of ground in the East End. 'Lazy Sunday', although sung in an exaggerated cockney accent, was actually written about Marriott's neighbours in Chiswick Walk, near the Thames in West London, where he had moved in 1967.

Although the band continued to have hits in 1967 and 1968, they started to suffer from a complaint that afflicted a number of the older established bands. By the end of 1967 you had to be a 'rock' band, with all that that entailed – musical dexterity,

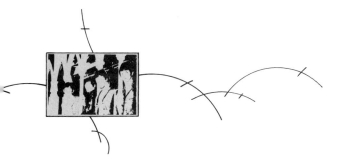

ninety-minute sets, etc. It was no longer good enough to write well-crafted pop songs. The public saw the Small Faces as anachronistic little mods, a plight not helped by the band themselves who, by late 1967, played so rarely in public that it was usually a disaster. They gave their last performance on New Year's Eve 1968, with Marriott storming offstage before the end.

Although all the members went on to bigger things in the 1970s (Marriott to Humble Pie, the rest to the Faces with Rod Stewart), that sparkle the Small Faces possessed, not to mention the Marriott-Lane writing team, was lost for good.

Before leaving East London, a word on the local Dagenham scene, centred around a pub called the Round House in Lodge Avenue. Dagenham had been a heavy rock and roll area in the 1950s and remained so well into the 1960s. One band from the area who played at the Round House, and went on to slightly bigger things, were Brian Poole and the Tremeloes. They started in the late 1950s, Poole doing a sort of Buddy Holly act complete with black-rimmed glasses. Later, when Merseybeat swept the country, the band adroitly switched styles, claiming they'd played that way all along. Although they had hits for a couple of years, it was obvious they had no special talents. Poole left in 1966 to start a solo career, which fizzled out very quickly. The Tremeloes were more successful on their own, although most 'serious' pop fans considered them a bad joke, especially when they announced that they were going 'progressive' in 1967. Poole himself returned to the family butcher's shop in the Romford Road, E12. In the last couple of years the band have reformed to play the 1960s revival and 'chicken-in-a-basket' circuit.

The Round House remained a venue, on and off, throughout the 1960s. Right at the end of the decade it became a 'progressive' club called The Village, which one night in April 1969 featured Led Zeppelin, playing almost their last English club date.

43. The Small Faces outside their Pimlico residence, late 1966.

BOWIE AND THE KINKS –
ROCK IN NORTH AND SOUTH LONDON
C H A P T E R S E V E N

**SILVER BLADES
ICE RINK
STREATHAM**

Monday evening next, 5th October
during the normal skating session

Personal appearances
THE PRETTY THINGS
THE BO STREET RUNNERS
supported by Tony Daryl in
"Spin of the Discs"

Doors open 6.45 p.m.
Admission 5/-

Advertisement for Streatham
Ice Rink.

South London has always seemed somewhat nebulous in music terms. There have always been clubs south of the river, but never any real scene. Although many fine musicians have come from South London, there have been few South London bands, as such. Certainly not in the way that the Who were always described as 'West London' and the Small Faces 'East London'. The 'South London Sound' didn't come of age until the late 1970s, with Squeeze.

From the earliest days, however, there was always somewhere to play. One of the first rock and roll venues anywhere in London was the Granada, Tooting. On a Sunday afternoon, bands (usually Larry Parnes' stable again) would appear between films. For many of the bands it was their first (and often their last) appearance on a big stage. The audience was composed almost entirely of hardcore South London teddy boys, regarded by many as the most vicious in London.

For many years the top promoter in the area was John Hopping, very much the equivalent, south of the river, of Alex King. Hopping ran a number of venues including the Dolphin on Streatham High Road, nearly opposite the Silver Blades Ice Rink (itself a venue for many years), which existed throughout

44. David Bowie onstage with the Konrads, 1963.

Advertisement for the Bromel Club, 1964.

the early 1960s and was popular with the more 'soul' orientated bands like Georgie Fame and the Blue Flames. If you went through a Friday night without a fight, it was a miracle. Everything got completely smashed. These days it's a little more upmarket, called (something like) the Purple Pussycat and is known in the area as a 'villain's' night out. For several years Hopping also promoted gigs at the Surrey Rooms at the Oval, SE11. This was always a successful venue and was still going in the late 1960s, putting on the usual mixture of soul, blues and progressive music.

The Beat/R n B boom of 1963–5 saw a number of popular clubs in South-east London. The Glenlyn (Waldram Road, SE23) has already been mentioned in the Who section. In its early days, it was one of the clubs the up and coming provincial bands played as one of their 'big' London dates. Slightly later it settled down as one of the regular venues on the London R n B circuit.

Also out in South-east London was the Bromel Club, which operated at least two venues simultaneously: Sundays through Thursdays at the Bromley Court Hotel, Bromley Hill, Kent; Fridays and Saturdays, the Co-op Hall, Rye Lane, Peckham, SE15.

Bromley has (as one might hope) a bigger claim to fame than the Bromel Club. It was also the town in which future superstar David Bowie grew up. Technically Bowie (or as he then was, Jones) was born in Brixton, but all his teenage years were spent in Bromley. He attended Bromley Technical High School and by his mid-teens was leading his own band (George and the Dragons) as a sax player, after which he joined another band, the Konrads, also on sax.

Legend has it that one day in late 1963 Bowie was waiting to have his hair cut at the local barber's in Bromley. Also waiting were four other musicians; together they became Davie Jones and the King Bees, a sub-Rolling Stones outfit, who managed one single before disbanding.

1965 saw Bowie fronting the Mannish Boys, the rest of whom came from Maidstone, prompting one local reviewer to suggest the arrival of 'The Medway Sound'. By 1966, with his name changed to Bowie (after confusion over David Jones of the Monkees), he was fronting yet another band, the Lower Third, and playing regularly at the Marquee. Despite further singles, fame eluded Bowie, who by the end of 1966 was recording as a soloist. During 1968 he worked with mime artist Lindsay Kemp and then, in the summer of 1969, success finally came with the 'Space Oddity' single.

Bowie had long since moved away from Bromley to Central London, first to a flat at 39 Manchester Street, W1 and later to Gunter Grove, SW10. However, much inspired by the underground/hippy activities of the previous two years, he then moved back to suburban Kent, to open the Beckenham Arts Lab.

The original Arts Lab was in Drury Lane, Covent Garden, run by two veterans of the London underground, Jim Haynes and Jack Henry Moore. It opened in 1968 and was conceived as something radically different, even from other underground clubs like UFO. It featured drama, underground films and experimental music, and it also had an art gallery, a restaurant and a book stall. Haynes himself pioneered the use of video at the Arts Lab. Rock groups occasionally performed there but they were generally unknown bands who played for nothing. Bowie (and his own short-lived mime group, Feathers) performed there a number of times in the summer of 1968, without much success, but Bowie was so impressed with the ideals and energy of the place that he decided to start one himself.

He wasn't alone in this. In late 1968 and throughout 1969 Arts Labs sprang up all over the country – Manchester, Swindon, Brighton. There was even one in the less than arty West London suburb of Hounslow, which convened at the White Bear pub in Kingsley Road. The ideas of their founders were similar to Haynes', but their clientèle (largely second- or third-generation hippies) were more interested in rock bands,

45. Bowie song writing in London Park, 1966.

notably the Edgar Broughton Band, whose song 'Out Demons Out' became a virtual anthem at these places.

Bowie opened the Beckenham Arts Lab, in a room over the Three Tuns pub in the High Street, in early 1969. For a while it went very well and became the centre of Bowie's life. In an interview in mid-1969 he said, 'Arts Labs should be for everyone, not just the so-called "turned-on" minority . . . Here we are in Beckenham with a group of people creating their own momentum without the slightest concern for attitudes . . . It's alive, healthy and new and matters to me more than anything else.' For a while the multimedia aspect of the Arts Lab flourished, with Bowie a constant, but far from the only, source of energy. Gradually, however, from the time that 'Space Oddity' became a hit, more and more people came solely to see Bowie perform, usually an acoustic set at the start of an evening. At the end of the year, Bowie and his new girlfriend Angie found themselves a place to live in Beckenham that seemed like a perfect offshoot of the Arts Lab ambience. It was called Haddon Hall, a huge, rambling Victorian folly complete with a ballroom and turrets. The fact that Bowie only rented a flat in the place and that his address, technically, was Flat 7, 42 Southend Road, Beckenham, did not deter him from using Haddon Hall as part of the letter-head on his correspondence.

By the middle of 1970 the Arts Lab had folded, with Bowie disillusioned by the numbers of people just wanting to see him rather than participate. A single of the time, 'Memories of Free Festival', summed up the energy and excitement of the best of the Arts Lab period, and it also pointed to the future. It was Bowie's first record in years that used a rock band. It signalled the return of Bowie as a rock performer, back on the circuit and on the first stage of the road to megastardom.

The years 1964–7 were the period of pirate radio. Clubs frequently became associated with one or other of the stations, who in turn promoted special club nights. One such in South-east London was the Witchdoctor, in Rushey Green,

Catford, allied with Radio London, which also broadcast from the club. Regular DJ Dave Cash (now on Capital Radio) had pioneered the catch-phrase 'Hello Myrtle', to which the reply was 'Hello Dear'. At the Witchdoctor this was transformed into 'Hello Catford', with the audience shouting the response.

The Croydon area also boasted a couple of good clubs during this period. The best known was the Star Hotel on the London Road, which in 1964 became one of Giorgio Gomelsky's Crawdaddy Clubs, which flourished following the success of the original club in Richmond. Not surprisingly the club frequently presented Gomelsky's acts, like Garry Farr and the T. Bones and the Yardbirds. The Yardbirds were also popular just down the road at the Kazzoo Klub (located in the Wallington Public Hall), where the resident band in late 1964–5 was the Herd. Originally an R n B band, the Herd made a few good but unsuccessful singles. In early 1967 they were joined by Peter Frampton, who had attended the same school as Bowie. In fact, although several years younger, Frampton had been in the rival school group, the Little Ravens. With Frampton, the Herd became a more overtly pop orientated band and started having hits. The success ultimately led to their demise, with Frampton suffering the misfortune of being described as 'the face of '68' and their records becoming not just commercial but banal; the band broke up in a fit of musical integrity. Although they all went on to other bands, Frampton was the only one to become a genuine rock star, first with Humble Pie (the band he formed with Steve Marriott) and later as a solo artist.

As already noted in earlier chapters, by 1966 a distinct polarisation was taking place in the London music scene: on the one hand, the art school R n B folk movement; on the other, the hardcore soul fraternity. Such generalisations are always dangerous. In some ways the gap had always been there and in some senses it was arbitrary because there were people who moved (certainly in terms of image/fashion) from one camp to the other and back. None the less, by 1966 the divisions were definitely clearer: in the suburbs, in particular, the split took on geographical as well as social dimensions. The heavily built-up working-class areas tended to be 'soul' strongholds. In urban South London this was certainly the case, where the most popular club of the era was the Ram Jam, located at 390 Brixton Road, London SW9.

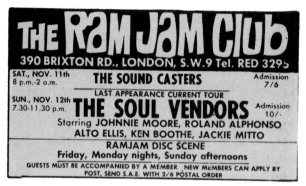

1967.

In fact the Ram Jam had a reputation that spread far beyond Brixton and was probably the most famous pure soul club in the country. The club name derived from the Ram Jam Band, a group fronted by Geno Washington, a black ex-GI who had been stationed in England. Between 1965 and 1968 Geno was the king of English soul music. The chant of 'Geno, Geno' was heard in clubs all over the country, yet despite the idolatry his success was confined almost entirely to live venues. The excitement of his act never transferred on to record, partly because his set consisted almost entirely of cover versions — by 1966, 'original' songs had become almost a prerequisite of commercial success. When their source material began to dry up with the decline of soul music in the States, the Ram Jam

Band's days were numbered. By late 1968 they had folded.

With the arrival of the blues boom in 1967, South London had at least one club devoted to it – the Blue Horizon Club, located at the Nag's Head pub, 205 York Road, Battersea, which opened in September 1967. The club was run by Mike Vernon, whose contribution to the growth of the blues in Britain was almost as significant as any of the more famous musicians. In 1964 Vernon had started the seminal R n B Monthly (a magazine that covered all aspects of the genre) and at the same time he joined Decca as an assistant producer. For Decca he went on to compile a number of definitive blues albums from American backlist record catalogues, as well as signing and producing many English acts, his most notable success being the John Mayall/Eric Clapton 'Bluesbreakers' album in 1966. In 1965 Vernon had started his own label, Blue Horizon, initially as a small-time mail-order venture, aimed entirely at collectors and real fans. With the growing popularity of the blues, Blue Horizon was suddenly a viable proposition and when the newly formed Fleetwood Mac signed, it became a fully-fledged, nationally distributed enterprise. The club, of course, took its name from the label, and it was no surprise that Fleetwood Mac played on the opening night. The early resident band at the club were the Boilerhouse Blues Band, who featured a very young guitar player called Danny Kirwan. Subsequently Kirwan joined Fleetwood Mac and stayed with them through their first (and arguably best) phase. Their leader, Peter Green, was probably the best blues guitarist in the country, yet he also managed to write excellent songs like 'Oh Well' and 'The Green Manalishi', that were commercial hits and hardly blues-based at all. (It should be pointed out that the Fleetwood Mac of the late 1960s bears little relation musically to the superstars of the late 1970s.)

The earliest venues in North London were trad jazz places. Some of them, like Cook's Ferry Inn in Edmonton, started putting on music shortly after the war. During the early 1950s, Cook's Ferry Inn was the home base of the Freddie Randall Band. It was also one of the regular haunts of all the early British jazz bands, including Mick Mulligan's, whose singer George Melly recalled: 'To reach the Ferry was a considerable labour. You caught the tube to Finsbury Park and then there was a long bus ride through the depressing suburbs with their chain stores and second-hand car lots on the bomb sites. Finally there were half-hearted fields and factories . . . and then a bridge over the canal in the style of the city of the future in the film "Things To Come". The ferry was on the far bank of this canal, a big 1935 pub in Brewers' Georgian with a hall attached. Its isolation had its advantages. The canal tow-path and the surrounding fields were suitable for knee-tremblers and yet you could still hear the band.' In the 1960s the Ferry remained a jazz venue, but like many others started featuring R n B; on these nights it was called the Blue Opera Club.

Other early jazz venues went over to R n B in 1963. One of the first was the Fishmonger's Arms, **287 High Road, Wood Green. Apparently, though, the venue's idea of R n B excluded anything approaching rock and roll. If a band played even Chuck Berry numbers (whose songs were definitely at the R n B end of rock) they were unlikely to be booked. In the late 1960s, however, the venue was used by a 'progressive' rock club, known as the 'Village of the Damned' who booked the major 'heavy' bands of the day, like Stray and the Edgar Broughton Band.**

Slightly south of the Fishmonger's was another popular pub-style venue, the Manor House, **opposite the tube station of the same name. The promoter there, Ron Leslie, went for R n B and the blues in a big way, the club becoming known as** Bluesville. **During the blues boom in 1969, Leslie opened further 'Bluesvilles' at the** Hornsey Wood Tavern **in the Seven Sisters Road, N4 and the Cherry Tree out in Welwyn Garden City.**

Another long-running venue was Klook's Kleek **at the**

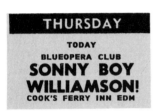

Advertisement for the Blue Opera Club, 1964.

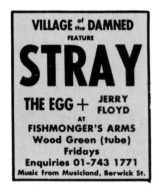

Railway Hotel in West Hampstead, run by Dick Jordan. Jordan attempted to put on a wide variety of jazz and R n B, but in November 1964 he was forced to drop modern jazz as it was no longer financially viable. Klook's was always known for its friendly and enthusiastic crowd and it's not surprising that a number of live albums were recorded there, by John Mayall and Zoot Money among others.

Although Klook's had closed by the end of the decade, Dick Jordan revived the name when he promoted a series of gigs in the West End, entitled 'Klook's at the Lyceum', which began in July 1970.

46. The Railway Hotel, West Hampstead, as it is today.

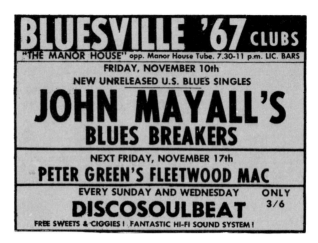

1967.

Slightly north-west of Klook's Kleek was another popular but now largely forgotten club called the Refectory, which was situated on the Finchley Road, near the Golders Green tube station. It was another jazz club that went over to R n B, although in this case the owners were Irish and on Friday nights it became an Irish dance hall. Perhaps the major event in the relatively short life of the Refectory took place on a freezing night in December 1966, when members paid the princely sum of ten shillings to see the only British appearance (other than Ready Steady Go!) of the Paul Butterfield Blues Band (featuring the late Mike Bloomfield on guitar). They performed for well under an hour, through a less than wonderful sound system, but it was a magical evening all the same. Why the band played only this one (and indeed, unlikely) gig is not known. The Refectory closed (except for the Irish dances) shortly after.

Not far from Hampstead Heath, elsewhere in North London, was the Country Club, located on Haverstock Hill, near Belsize Park. The Country Club retained a jazz-only policy longer than most other venues, but by the end of the decade was regarded as one of the best progressive rock clubs in London. Some of Fairport Convention's most success-ful gigs were played at the Country Club and many other bands of the era have fond memories of the place.

The North London clubs described so far attracted primarily, though by no means exlusively, a middle-class clientèle and certainly both the Country Club and Klook's Kleek were located in middle-class areas. But there was one North London club which differed on both counts – the Club Noreik in Seven Sisters Road in Tottenham. Between 1964 and 1966 the Noreik was the leading mod club in north London. The venue, a large old cinema, was run by Alex Jack, an agent who booked bands for US air bases, stag nights or anything that made money. The club was relatively rare among suburban clubs in that it ran all-nighters, often with bands like the Who, or the local heroes, the Action.

The Action are worth mentioning as, despite a lack of com-mercial success, they were one of the most popular London bands, especially north of the river. The group formed in early 1964, playing initially at the Malden Arms, Malden Road, Kentish Town. On the point of breaking up they were offered the slot of backing band to a lady called Sandra Barry – the group became the Boyfriends, subsequently the Boys. The Boys split from Ms Barry and cut one single before becoming the Action. As the Action they became the leading exponents in London of the Tamla Motown style of soul music, acquiring a phenomenal mod following. They signed with Parlophone and were produced by Beatle producer George Martin. Unfortunately commercial success eluded them, primarily because, as with Geno Washington, their act was based too heavily on covers of US material. By 1968 they started writing their own material, but by then it was too late. They were joined by Martin Stone, one of the best and most underrated guitar players in Britain. At this point they abandoned their soul roots almost completely and moved towards a West Coast, guitar-based, acid rock sound. They also changed their name to Mighty Baby, one of the best remembered (if again uncommercial) bands of the late 1960s.

To return, briefly, to the Club Noreik. The club failed to outlive the mod era, but the premises survived until quite recently, finally being torn down at the end of 1984.

The Noreik, as noted, was in Tottenham, and it's impossible to mention the suburb without some reference to the Dave Clark 5, prime (and indeed sole) exponents of what was described, albeit briefly, as the 'Tottenham Sound'. The band formed as a skiffle group (rather late in the day) in 1959, but by 1962 they had gone electric, playing their first gig as a pop group at the South Grove Youth Club in Tottenham. In early 1963 they became the featured second act at the Tottenham Royal Ballroom, where they were spotted and signed up by a Columbia Records talent scout. The 'Tottenham Sound' tag came with the success of their third single, 'Glad All Over', in November 1963. The idea was to promote them as London's answer to the Beatles and Merseybeat, but most people saw through the hype and within a few months it was obvious that the real answer to Liverpool lay in the London R n B bands, especially the Stones. The Dave Clark 5's music was essentially straight pop with a heavy, if rather monotonous, beat; their act, as one critic described it, was 'mechanical and lifeless'. The band were never really part of the club scene described in this book; they moved almost straight out of the Royal and on to nationwide package tours. Their popularity in Britain had faded considerably by the end of 1964, but it's fair to say that they remained hugely popular in the States for several years.

For most people, however, the definitive North London band of the era were the Kinks. Arguably, they started off as an archetypal 'North London' group. Then, as they became more successful, they became the archetypal 'London' band. Finally, by the late 1960s, they'd become (especially to Americans) the archetypal 'British' band.

The Kinks were the brainchild of two brothers, Ray and Dave Davies, the youngest of a large family who lived in Fortis Green, on the borders of Muswell Hill (later immortalised by the band on the 'Muswell Hillbillies' album in 1971) and Highgate. The brothers were interested in music from an early age and by the time they were in their early teens and attending the William Grimshaw Secondary School in Muswell Hill, they were both playing guitar and listening to the blues. Although too young even to enter a pub, the brothers were already playing their first gigs, at the Clissold Arms, across the road from where they lived in Fortis Green. They played as an acoustic duo, influenced primarily by the records of Big Bill Broonzy. Despite the fact that both brothers hated school, it was there that the first incarnation of the Kinks came into being. Also in Ray's year were Peter Quaife, an aspiring guitar player, and John Start, would-be drummer. They became (amongst other things) the Ray Davies Quartet, playing locally for anyone who would pay them.

At the end of 1962 Ray went off to Hornsey Art School, where he heard Alexis Korner's band for the first time. It was Korner who suggested that if Ray wanted to join an R n B band he should talk to Giorgio Gomelsky. At the time Gomelsky was running a blues club called the Piccadilly Club, at 41 Great Windmill Street (the much-used premises that had previously been the Cy Laurie club and was later to be the Scene), where the resident group were the Dave Hunt R n B Band (see also Chapter 2). Davies joined as guitarist, but was more interested in the style and image of the band that were playing Hunt's intervals, the Rolling Stones. Davies played with Hunt for several months, while brother Dave kept the band together in Muswell Hill. Ray played with them as and when he could, such as a gig at Hornsey Town Hall (A 'St Valentine's Day Carnival Dance'), February 1963. They were called various things – the Ray Davies Quartet, the Bo-Weevils and the Ravens. Ray left Hornsey that summer and coincidentally the Hunt band broke up. This was followed by a brief and half-hearted few months at the Croydon School of Art, but by the late autumn Ray had permanently rejoined the others back in Muswell Hill.

There then followed an odd stage of their careers. They acquired two upper-class managers, one of whom, Robert Wace, aspired to being a singer, so the Bo-Weevils/Ravens became his backing band. This period saw them playing debs' parties, hunt balls and unlikely venues like the Worshipful Company of Grocers' Hall, in Princes Street, EC2. Their general appearance, which also included a lot of leather and thigh length boots, led to them being described as 'kinky' (a vogue word at the time). In short order they became the Kinks.

By this time (still early 1964), Wace had wisely adopted a purely managerial role and the group itself had found a new drummer, Mick Avory, whose major claim to fame was that the previous summer he'd turned down an offer to join the embryonic Rolling Stones. They were also signed to Pye Records, who presumably hoped to get a band to rival the Stones. They didn't have long to wait. August 1964 saw the first of Ray Davies' many reworkings of that most basic rock and roll number, the Kingsmen's 'Louie Louie', entitled 'You Really Got Me'. It was a massive hit, the first of many.

The Kinks were still very much an R n B band, but subtly different from the Stones or any of the other groups. After the first hit the Kinks rarely played the club circuit again, concentrating on rather dreadful package tours. None the less they retained their London roots. Dave and Mick, for example, shared a flat in Connaught Gardens, Muswell Hill, throughout the early days. In general their relationship with London was never doubted, and as the Carnaby Street photo-sessions testify, they were very much part of 'Swinging London'.

By 1966 it was obvious that Ray was developing a unique songwriting talent. The simplistic (though effective) 'Louie Louie' reworkings were replaced by delightful vignettes and witty social commentaries. 'Dedicated Follower of Fashion' (from February 1966) remains the definitive satire of the Carnaby Street poseur, whilst the elegiac 'Waterloo Sunset' (May 1967) is one of the finest songs ever written about London.

47. The Kinks model their new
    hunting outfits, the imme-
    diate (somewhat toned
    down) successors to the
    'Kinky' leather gear,
    autumn 1964.

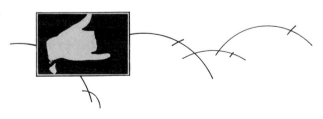

48. The Kinks performing 'Dedicated Follower of Fashion' on TV, February 1966.

BOWIE AND THE KINKS

The period from 1966 to the end of 1968 was the Kinks' finest, Ray seeming equally happy to write about the upper classes ('Sunny Afternoon') and the working class ('Dead End Street', although technically this was written about the eighteen-month period Ray and his wife spent in a tiny Muswell Hill flat). Towards the end of the 1960s, Ray became increasingly obsessed with a mythical golden age of English life that had vanished with the First World War. 'The Village Green Preservation Society' album was the culmination of his ideas.

Although it lies outside the period of this book, Davies did return to writing about his roots, with the 'Muswell Hillbillies' album in late 1971. The album cover shows the band drinking in the Archway Tavern, Holloway, and prancing around nearby Retcar Close.

The Kinks are still with us, along with the Stones virtually the only surviving band from the early 1960s. The Kinks' songs are generally not what they were 18 years ago, but once in a while, when everybody has written them off, Ray comes back with another hit single of quality and insight. Ironically, as one of the few enduring rockers to show any sign of remembering his own rock roots, Davies and his band now enjoy a far wider following in the US than on their home ground.

LONDON SWINGS, 1964–6
C H A P T E R   E I G H T

When Beatlemania struck at the Palladium in late 1963, it took the majority of the population by surprise. They were simply unaware that since the 1950s things had been changing, particularly in London. Suddenly every newspaper in the country wanted to find out who these kids were, what they did and, in some cases, why they were allowed to get away with it. Slowly but surely the press found out about the music, the clubs and the fashions. They never quite got it right, but then they never do. It didn't matter – however negative the publicity, it had one effect: it led to the massive spread of teen culture; 'pop style' had arrived. The media required a single symbol (other than the Beatles) to represent what was happening. One day it dawned on them – Carnaby Street.

Back in the 1950s Carnaby Street had simply been one of many tiny Soho back streets. It was comprised mainly of rag-trade sweat shops and a Central Electricity Board Depot, which took up most of one side. Sometime in the mid-1950s a gentleman by the name of Vince set up a photographic studio just off Carnaby Street and in due course started to design outfits for his (male) models. Until the early 1960s gays were about the only males in England, aside from West Indians, who wore brightly-coloured clothes and Vince found his creations were becoming a saleable commodity. However, because the gay population was fairly small, business was

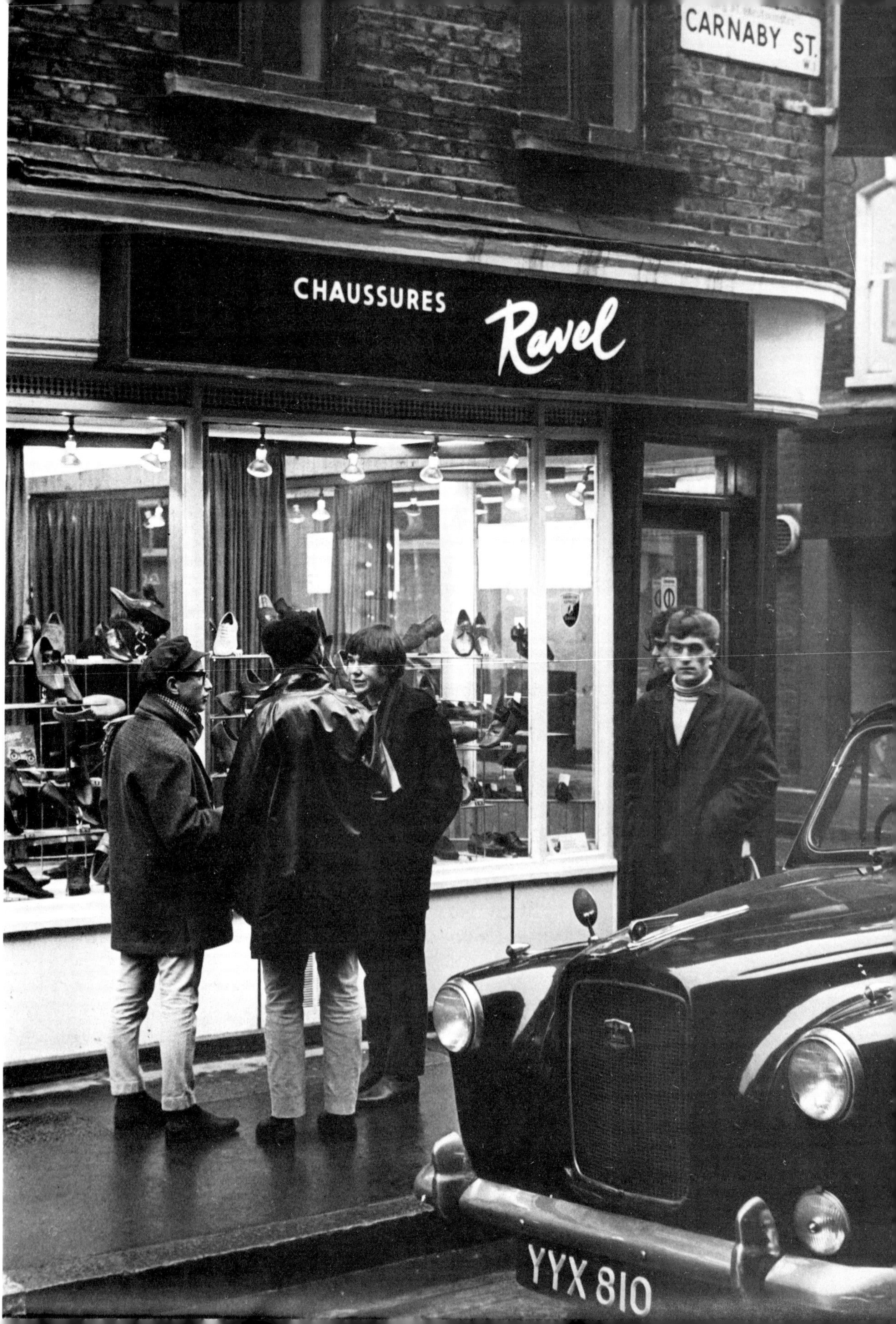
CARNABY ST.
CHAUSSURES
Ravel
YYX 810

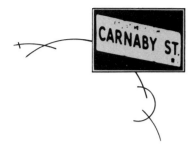

hardly booming. By the late 1950s, however, another group started to frequent his premises – mods, or, as they called themselves at the time, 'modernists' – who had previously gone to obscure specialist tailors in the East End for their outfits.

Around this time one of Vince's apprentice cutters, John Stephen, set up on his own and moved into Carnaby Street. Gradually other shops opened up and by the middle of 1962 there were four or five selling a mixture of 'made to measure' articles and American garments like Levi jeans and Ivy League shirts. With the increasing popularity of clubs like the Flamingo and the Scene, Carnaby Street started to become a mandatory stopping-off point for suburban kids 'up West'.

When the media found Carnaby Street, all hell broke loose. By the middle of 1964 all but about two of the premises were clothes shops or, to use the new word the press had discovered, 'boutiques'. For a while it really was a special place; much more than just a street of shops, it was a place to be seen. All the new pop groups bought their clothes there – and were naturally photographed doing so.

But as is the way with these things, the original spirit got lost somewhere along the way. By 1965 most of the privately owned boutiques, which made their own clothes, had gone, partly because the atmosphere had changed and partly because rents had sky-rocketed. They were replaced by 'chain-store' boutiques; their clientèle, instead of being top mods or people like Brian Jones or Eric Clapton, were tourists from the provinces or abroad. But along the way a major revolution had been effected – London, as we were constantly told, was 'swinging'.

Of course, London had been 'swinging' for years, but a sweaty cellar club full of beatniks was not everyone's idea of fun. In London, at least, it was the whole mod phenomenon that had changed everything, particularly after the first flush of Beatlemania had died. You couldn't be a Beatle, but you could be a mod, or at least something approaching one.

49. Carnaby Street, c.1965, pre-pedestrianisation.

'Mod' was undoubtedly a marketable commodity. Marketing the fashions was a piece of cake after the rise of Carnaby Street; marketing its other aspects, notably the music, had to be more subtle. Everything still worked on two levels: the genuine article and the watered-down commercial variant. The clubs, for example, remained the least unsullied, despite their massive proliferation during 1964 and 1965. The London club scene was, at the time, the best and the biggest in the world.

For those in the know, the London club scene was where you found out what was going on – the latest bands, the latest American sounds, new fashions, etc. But for those who didn't visit the clubs, especially those who lived out of London, they needed other ways to keep in touch, which meant radio and TV.

Prior to Easter 1964, radio had been totally in the hands of the BBC and Radio Luxembourg – the BBC still clung to its 'Auntie' image and rarely played pop music. Even worse, because of its 'needle-time' restrictions, the BBC also never played anything that wasn't safe and commercial. Luxembourg played more pop, but since the four major record labels bought about 95 per cent of the available air time, not a lot else was heard. All of that changed at Easter 1964 when the first pirate ship, Radio Caroline, went on the air. With no needle-time problems, and a desire to play any of the new music being heard around the London clubs, irrespective of source, it was a major breakthrough. Other stations followed, notably Radio London, which appropriately enough was the most popular in the London area.

Although obviously not based in London, the stations, particularly Radio London, had a symbiotic relationship with London music and the clubs. The stations played the music from the clubs and by so doing increased interest in both the music and the clubs themselves. Also, despite their dubious legality, the stations took to running clubs around town or at

50. Tiles club, Oxford Street, 1966.

least sponsoring nights at established clubs. Radio London, for example had the Starlight Ballroom in Greenford and Radio Caroline used Tiles in Oxford Street. These events provided publicity and raised funds for the stations. In return, the punters were able to see some of the otherwise faceless DJs.

51. Cathy McGowan interviewing Mick Jagger on *Ready Steady Go!* 1964.

Throughout their three-and-a-half year lifespan (they were finally outlawed in the summer of 1967), the pirates did a remarkable job in promoting individual artists and musical styles that would never have taken off otherwise. They could not, however, recreate the atmosphere and visual excitement of the music or the new styles and images of the era, which is where TV came in, in the shape of Ready Steady Go!. RSG! had started in August 1963, but for the first few months seemed uncertain as to what it was trying to do. By mid-1964 it had established its own style and from then until its demise in late 1966 it was the pop TV programme, required viewing for anyone remotely interested in pop culture. Despite its inevitable commercial trappings (you can't get much more 'overground' than prime-time network ITV) it seemed to spring straight out of the London clubs. It was exciting, great to look at (they borrowed ideas for set designs from the leading 'pop artists' like Derek Boshier and Peter Blake) and the audience looked unusually 'genuine'. In fact the audience was usually selected from the best dancers at the Scene club. Unlike tired old Top Of The Pops, which concentrated on groups already in the charts, RSG! featured acts unknown outside the London club circuit. Thus you could see the Who, the Yardbirds, the Small Faces, Manfred Mann, not to mention the Stones and countless other groups before (in some cases) they even had a record out. They would also bring in groups from the States, like the Beach Boys and the Byrds or R n B acts like Inez and Charlie Foxx, whose records were big at the Scene, but until RSG! meant nothing to someone in Scunthorpe.

RSG! was also paramount in spreading fashion consciousness and ideas on style. People would tune in to find out what they should be wearing; it became almost as important as the music.

For many observers, the programme's female host, Cathy McGowan, became the embodiment of 'swinging London'. Lifted from total obscurity, she became, in a matter of months, a national celebrity.

52. Ultra-hip follower of fashion grooving the night away at the Scotch of St James club, late 1966.

53. The exterior of the Cromwellian Club, as it is today.

This new 'classlessness' was supposed to be the core of swinging London. It was now possible, so they said, for the working classes to rub shoulders with the aristocracy in a new classless society. In fact, for many people, the 1960s in general, and swinging London in particular, are summed up by the Beatles and dolly birds in mini-skirts driving around in Mini-mokes with the younger sons of the aristocracy. This is largely a myth, but the extent to which it did happen is worth investigating.

From about the beginning of 1964 a number of clubs opened in London to cater for the youngbloods of the gentry who had discovered pop music, where they could mix with the new 'working-class aristocracy'. Primarily this meant successful pop musicians plus a few other newly acceptable professions, notably photographers and fashion designers plus a few actors, artists and the odd East End gangster.

The clubs, despite the 'classless' pop music, were expensive and very elitist. The most popular was the Ad-Lib, located in a penthouse in Leicester Place just off Leicester Square, which opened in February 1964. Previously it had been an unsuccessful club called Wips, but the new owners had brought in John Kennedy, Tommy Steele's first manager, to run the club. He installed low tables and amplification and turned it into a disco. John Lennon was their first catch, then Ringo. After that they were turning people away. For a while, at least, every self-respecting pop star in London would drop in after a gig or on a night off.

With the success of the Ad-Lib, various rivals opened up. The Scotch of St James, situated near St James's Square, was opened by two mysterious gentlemen, a Mr Brown and a Mr Bloom, but the host was Rod Harrod, a well-known man about town at the time. Decked out in Scottish baronial style, it still managed to attract the likes of Mick Jagger.

Then there was (and to some extent still is) the Cromwellian, located in a big Georgian house on the Cromwell Road, in South Kensington. The Cromwellian featured live music as

well as a disco — if you could afford it. Georgie Fame and Zoot Money were frequently on the bill. They were also regulars at two other clubs, slightly less upmarket, owned by the Gunnells, who also owned the Flamingo. The first was the Revolution, in Bruton Place, Mayfair, which was a popular place for record company parties, a notable night being the one when a reception was held there for Country Joe and the Fish in 1967. The other Gunnell club was the Bag O'Nails in Bond Street, which was slightly more approachable than the Revolution, although run on the same lines and featuring the same sort of bands. Both were somewhat upmarket versions of the Flamingo.

Fascinating though these clubs were, they were never really representative of what was happening in London, but from a newspaper's point of view they were understandably more glamorous than an all-nighter in a cellar club. It was the same upmarket side of things that tended to be portrayed in films. The prime example is Blow-Up, a supposedly accurate por-

54. Interior shot of the Cromwellian Club in full swing,
1966.

trayal of swinging London directed by Michelangelo Antonioni. Not only did it perpetuate the myth in all its inaccuracies but, as it wasn't released until early 1968, it seemed very anachronistic. The film is redeemed by an excellent performance by the Yardbirds in a studio mock-up of, oddly enough, the Windsor Ricky Tick, albeit transposed into Oxford Street.

Despite all the myths and commercialisation, the period from 1964–6 was the great flowering of English pop culture. Arguably, many of the bands lost some of their roots and their raw edge when they became successful, but at the same time, being less purist made their music more approachable. It meant, if nothing else, that for nearly three years, really good music got into the charts.

By the end of 1966 things were changing, primarily because nothing in the pop world lasts for ever. The whole mod style was on the wane, RSG! had finished and musicians were becoming bored with the limitations of three-minute singles. It was time to move on.

55. David Hemmings as representative of swinging London's archetypal 'classless' profession — photographer. With Vanessa Redgrave in a still from *Blow-Up*.

THE UNDERGROUND
CHAPTER NINE

At the beginning of 1967, when the fashionable section of London's youth were socialising down at the Scotch and their less affluent brethren were still doing the all-nighter at the Flamingo, a whole new breed of both entertainers and entertained quietly sprang up – the 'underground'.

Of course, like most of the 'movements' examined in this book, the underground did not arrive overnight. In fact, the English underground had been around since the mid-1950s and consisted mainly of the people involved in the more avant garde activities mentioned in earlier chapters. Like its American counterpart (particularly in San Francisco) the founders of the supposedly 'new' mid-1960s underground were the poets, artists, bomb-banners, etc., who, apart from the occasional burst of notoriety over the previous decade, were virtually unknown to the public at large. All that was to change. By the summer of 1967 the underground was, to all intents and purposes, public property. There were various reasons for this. Although the media took little interest in a group of 30 people in a Soho basement attending an evening of avant garde poetry and jazz, they were fascinated/appalled by 10,000 people, supposedly high on LSD, wearing outrageous clothes, dancing to the weirdest rock music ever heard. That was news! It was the underground's absorption of 'rock' that proved to be the catalyst. The evolution of the underground is essentially the same as the evolution of the 'new' music and more specifically the clubs and events associated with it.

Perhaps not surprisingly, the first public manifestation of the phenomenon was actually a poetry event: the International Poetry Festival at the Royal Albert Hall in June 1965. The IPF brought together poets from the English alternative arts scene, like Pete Brown (later lyricist for Cream and a rock performer in his own right) and Americans such as Allen Ginsberg. The audience that day was full of strangely clad figures, bedecked with flowers and carrying joss sticks — hippies were making their first mass appearance in the UK.

A number of the Americans who helped organise the poetry event remained in London and became prime movers on the scene. One was Steve Stollman, brother of the owner of the avant garde ESP label in New York. In February 1966 he organised the first of a series of events known as 'Spontaneous Underground', which were held at the Marquee Club on Sunday afternoons. In retrospect these events seem oddly parochial, decidedly naive and closer to early 1960s beatnik happenings than anything else; they were, none the less, the first link in the chain that led to the UFO Club and beyond. The early ones featured artists like Pete Brown performing conjuring tricks, strange avant garde orchestras that utilised transistor radios, and, on one occasion, a girl playing a Bach fugue accompanied by African drummers. Then, in March 1966, Spontaneous Underground was enlivened by the appearance of an unknown band dubbed the Pink Floyd Sound. They were loud, weird and unique — and they fitted perfectly.

Over the weeks at the Marquee things developed, plans were hatched and the characters who were to become major forces in the underground — John Hopkins, Miles (who ran Indica Books), Andrew King and Pete Jenner (who became the Floyd's managers) and Joe Boyd — all came together. The scene shifted from the Marquee to the London Free School in

Notting Hill Gate, a community self-help establishment run primarily by 'Hoppy' (as Hopkins was universally known). One of its early classes was the Sound/Light Workshop, at which Pink Floyd often provided music. The group soon became the centre of interest, and All Saints Hall **in Powis Square was swamped every week. The stage was set for something new and exciting involving all the various components: lights, films, dance and music.**

The first big event of this 'new' underground was a party to launch International Times **(England's first underground paper and the brainchild of Miles and Hoppy), held at the** Roundhouse **in Chalk Farm on 15 October 1966. Originally an engine shed, the Roundhouse had been taken over by the Gilbey's Gin concern, which had installed a balcony that stood on wooden pillars. The building had a marvellous, almost romantic atmosphere – it was a monument to nineteenth-century industrial design. Unfortunately it was also cold, had almost no lighting, just two lavatories and the only entrance was via an ancient, steep and extremely narrow staircase.**

56. Exterior of the Roundhouse
(Chalk Farm) as it is today.

None the less the IT party was a memorable event. Some 2,000 people turned up and were greeted by Miles handing out sugar-cubes (which turned out not to be of the LSD-coated variety, despite hopeful rumour to the contrary). What took place set the style for later events: people in bizarre fancy dress rolling in huge jellies, dancing, revelling, tripping and watching films; a Bacchanal of the first order. Paul McCartney showed up dressed as an Arab, the Italian film director Michelangelo Antonioni was there taking a break from shooting Blow-Up and Marianne Faithfull, wearing a nun's habit, won the prize for the 'shortest barest' costume. Music was provided not only by Pink Floyd but also Soft Machine, whose instrumentation included a motorcycle with a contact mike attached to the cylinder head — the bike was revved up from time to time to add to the group's euphonious wailing.

Pink Floyd, meanwhile, brought with them the light show they had been using at the Free School — oil dropped on photographic slides pulsated in time with music. Within months that light show was to seem incredibly primitive, but few people had seen one before and the Roundhouse audience was transfixed. Musically the Floyd played one of their best sets, even though the power shortcircuited in the middle of 'Interstellar Overdrive'.

The IT party was also the first underground event to garner national press coverage: the Sunday Times ran a story on it, including an interview with Pink Floyd's Roger Waters. Over the next few weeks, further one-off events along the same lines took place. Some, like 'Psychodelphia Versus Ian Smith', were held at the Roundhouse; others, like the even more bizarrely-named 'Freak Out Ethel', were held elsewhere. However, none of them quite captured the magic of the IT party, especially as many (the 'New Year's Eve All Night Rave' at the Roundhouse, for example) were obviously commercially-motivated ventures. But by the end of the year, the underground had found a new centre — at UFO, the Friday night club founded by Hoppy (aided and abetted by Joe Boyd and Miles)

October 1966.

57. Soft Machine at UFO, 1967.

that had grown out of the Free School.

UFO was located in an Irish dance-hall called the Blarney Club in the basement of 32 Tottenham Court Road, opposite the Dominion Theatre, and opened on 23 December 1966. At first, the club was titled 'UFO Presents Night Tripper', the 'Night' part relevant as UFO always hosted all-night events, a factor that put it out of the reach of many hippies, especially young ones and those with day jobs.

The UFO legend has grown over the years and, as Roger Waters has said, 'It's got rosier with age, but there is a germ of truth in it.' So what actually happened there? It certainly wasn't just a club in the entertainment sense; it was a genuine meeting/market place for the underground. For the first couple of months virtually everyone knew everyone else who was packed inside and sniffed the overpowering aroma of sweat and dope; deals were made and projects planned. One could buy hippie paraphernalia from the 'head' shop or a frilly shirt from John Pearce's 'Granny Takes A Trip' stall. Later on, more intense activities took place in back rooms, like black activist Michael X relieving liberals of 'conscience' money for one of his schemes or Michael Henshaw (accountant to the underground and the responsible face of UFO) trying to arrange bail for someone. It was a remarkably relaxed environment, in which the likes of Mick Jagger or John Lennon could sit all night without being pestered for autographs.

And then there was the entertainment itself, with which UFO refined the previous mixed-media attempts into a heady brew that has never been equalled. Some nights it did bear more relation to the early 1960s – tired poets reading their works to the backing of jazz combos – but generally, especially when Pink Floyd played, it was magic. When UFO started, Hoppy had given the Floyd the contract to provide music and lights at the club. Although the group didn't play at UFO every week, it's fair to say that the club was home base for the band and it always gave them a chance to play for an audience that understood and loved their music.

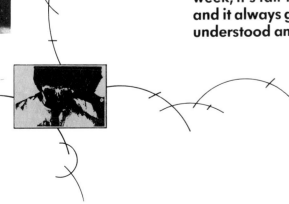

UFO also attracted many of the new bands who were springing up in the wake of the Floyd. Some went on to some degree of fame and fortune, notably Soft Machine, perhaps the most intellectual of them all. Others included Arthur Brown (he of the flaming head-dress), the Purple Gang (who recorded 'Granny Takes A Trip', a UFO anthem), Tomorrow (featuring singer Keith West, future Yes guitarist Steve Howe and a great line in theatrics) and Procul Harum, who played at UFO the week their 'A Whiter Shade Of Pale' went to number one.

Not everyone thought that UFO — or the underground in general — was wonderful, however. There was increasingly abusive coverage in the press, and at the beginning of April 1967 the police raided the offices of IT in a calculated attempt to close the paper down. In order to raise money, a benefit event was put together. 'The 14 Hour Technicolor Dream', as it was called, took place at Alexandra Palace on 29 April and it turned out to be the biggest single underground event ever — though it is a curious paradox that something that attracted

UFO

has moved to The Roundhouse; we realise that many members and friends had come to love the premises at 31 Tottenham Court Road, but we were unfortunately unable to accommodate all the people that wanted to come in.

We also realise that to many of our friends "ROUND-HOUSE" means a cold, uncomfortable place which has been the site of some unsuccessful "FREAK OUT" promotions in the past.

It is, however, now vastly improved in comfort and we tried it out with a private party for members only this past Friday night and concensus was that it was one of the best "UFOs" ever.

With more time to prepare the lighting this coming Friday's show with THE TOMORROW and The Chris Mc-Gregor Quintet should be very beautiful. Applications for new membership will also be available.

August 1967.

58. Part of the 10,000 crowd at the '14 Hour Technicolor Dream' held at the Alexandra Palace, April 1967.

59. Soft Machine at the '14
    Hour Technicolor Dream',
    April 1967.

over 10,000 people could be described as 'underground'. This immense crowd turned up to watch 41 bands, listen to poetry, see films and ride the helter-skelter. There were two stages with bands playing simultaneously. With the various light shows, there was almost too much to take in. Soft Machine were in top form — Kevin Ayers in cowboy hat surmounted by aeroplane wings, Daevid Allen in miner's helmet — but once again it was Pink Floyd who stole the show, coming on as the first light of dawn poured through the high windows, their eerie sounds echoing around the building. In retrospect, the Technicolor Dream was not only the biggest and best underground event, but also the last genuine one.

Back at UFO things were starting to go awry; basically it was too small to accommodate the increasing number of visitors. The original 'freaks' and hippies had been largely displaced by unwelcome newcomers: at best, these were 'weekend hippies', at worst they were drunken sailors (who took the idea of 'free love' a little too literally) or hippie-bashing skinheads.

The crunch came in June, when Hoppy was imprisoned for drug offences. Police pressure on the club increased in the weeks following, resulting in the landlords revoking the lease. The club moved into the Roundhouse but, despite the fact that the building was still almost derelict, the rent was exorbitant. When a big name like Eric Burdon or Jeff Beck was playing, UFO broke even, but the club more often lost money. The Roundhouse may have been a good place for special events, but the atmosphere of the club evaporated in the cold emptiness of the building. UFO stuck it out until October and then folded — for many people it was the end of an era.

That summer of 1967 had represented the height, in public terms, of the new alternative culture; by the autumn it had sunk, very nearly without trace. From being the property of a committed minority the previous winter, it had spread with remarkable speed throughout the country, falling prey to over-commercialisation; neck-bells tinkled in high streets

60. The Deviants formerly the Social Deviants) on the steps of St Paul's Cathedral, 1968.

across the country and by September flower power had become a national joke. The music suffered too. Any band that had been remotely associated with kaftans or bells was in danger of being laughed off stage.

Pockets of resistance held out, however, and a few clubs continued something approximating to a UFO style. UFO had not been the only club with an underground atmosphere and clientèle at the time, but the others were without exception more overtly commercial enterprises. One of the best was Happening 44, located at 44 Gerrard Street, W1 in Soho and run by Jack Bracelin, who had been part of the Free School Light/Sound workshop where he had developed his own light show. The Social Deviants (with future rock journalist and sometime novelist Mick Farren) were virtually Happening 44's houseband.

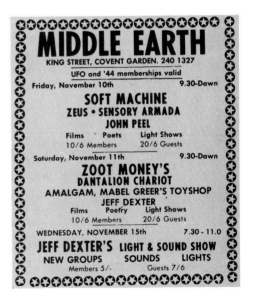

November 1967.

61. Exterior of 43 King Street, Covent Garden, 1968, the original home of Middle Earth. Entry into the club was via the little gate to the right of the main door.

Better known than Happening 44, however, was Middle Earth in Covent Garden. This had evolved from the Electric Garden which had opened a few months after UFO but, despite interesting bills, had never taken off. Yoko Ono was supposed to have sensed 'bad vibrations' on the opening night – possibly because the club was allegedly run by two East End gangsters. After a couple of months it closed and then reopened as Middle Earth. It was still run on commercial lines, but the new owners wisely employed hippies as organisers of the club, notably Dave Howson, who had been one of the organisers of the 'Technicolor Dream'. While UFO was still in operation, Middle Earth diplomatically closed on Friday nights.

After the demise of UFO, however, Middle Earth took over

as the main underground music club. The club's policy was, in some ways, less adventurous than that of UFO, but their more commercial nature meant they were able to book more big-name artists, especially from the United States; over the following year Tim Buckley, Captain Beefheart, the Byrds and even the Ike and Tina Turner Revue played in Covent Garden. Also, like UFO, Middle Earth tried out the Roundhouse for a few gigs, and pulled off a major coup in putting on Jefferson Airplane and the Doors in September 1968. Shortly after, however, the club folded – another victim of dwindling finances and police pressure. Arguably, Middle Earth was the last genuine underground club, although mention should be made of the Temple, which in 1969 operated out of the basement of the old Flamingo Club in Wardour Street. The Temple was probably the seediest rock venue London has ever had and attracted a clientèle to match: acid casualties, speed freaks, shysters and thieves. Its only redeeming feature was a huge mural behind the stage executed by Mal Dean, an artist who had been associated with the underground from the early 1960s.

Despite the general turning away from any music that was remotely flowery, the concept of the 'new' rock music had taken hold. Although there had been a division in the world of pop music, certainly since 1963, between, say, Jim Reeves and the Stones, by 1968 the divisions had become barriers, which remained in place until the late 1970s and the arrival of punk.

In every way the music had changed, for better and worse. On the plus side groups had started to demand the freedom to play the music they wanted and had begun to write and arrange their own material. Inevitably this led to a general shift away from three-minute singles towards albums. Quite justifiably they began to see themselves as 'rock musicians' rather than 'pop performers'. On both sides of the Atlantic, individuals became revered, not for their sex appeal or because they had top 10 singles, but because of their musical dexterity.

62. Pete Brown performing at
the Temple, 1969.

This, unfortunately, had a number of negative side-effects. Musicians tended to believe their own publicity, which in time led to the massively self-indulgent music of the early 1970s. On the other side of the speaker banks, audiences started to believe it as well. People stopped dancing and began sitting cross-legged on the floor, to gaze at the flying fingers of the lead guitar player. From there it was only one step up to the concert hall. If a barrier had developed between serious rock and kiddy pop, another one grew up between artist and audience.

Of course new artists couldn't play the Royal Albert Hall immediately, and for a time the club and dance hall circuits held on and even received impetus from the 'blues revival' of 1968–9. Even then things had obviously changed. Most of the audience were there to check out the sub-Peter Green guitarist, not to dance or because they had any interest in the blues.

By the end of 1969, the concept of real 'clubs', each with its own identity, had died; the Rick Ticks, Eel Pie Island and the Crawdaddy were long gone. Small gigs were simply the back rooms of pubs. Many clubs had used pub premises, but only out of convenience, and there the club atmosphere prevailed – almost by default.

Few people mourned the decline of the London clubs but it's interesting that they virtually vanished with the passing of the 1960s. If one regards the 1960s as a very special era, rather than just a block of ten years, perhaps the decline of the London club scene along with the decade should come as no surprise.

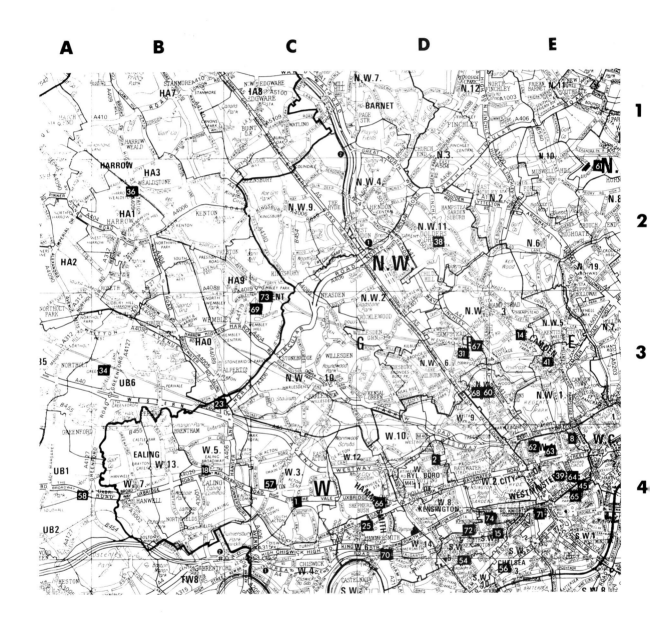

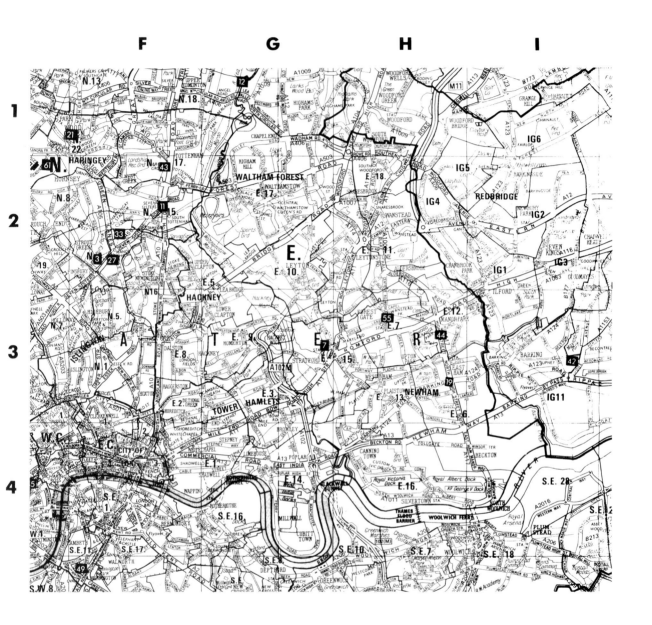

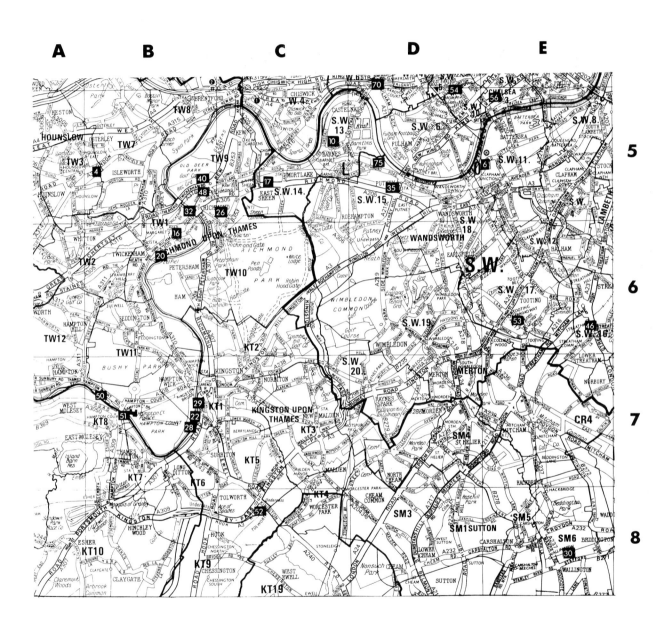

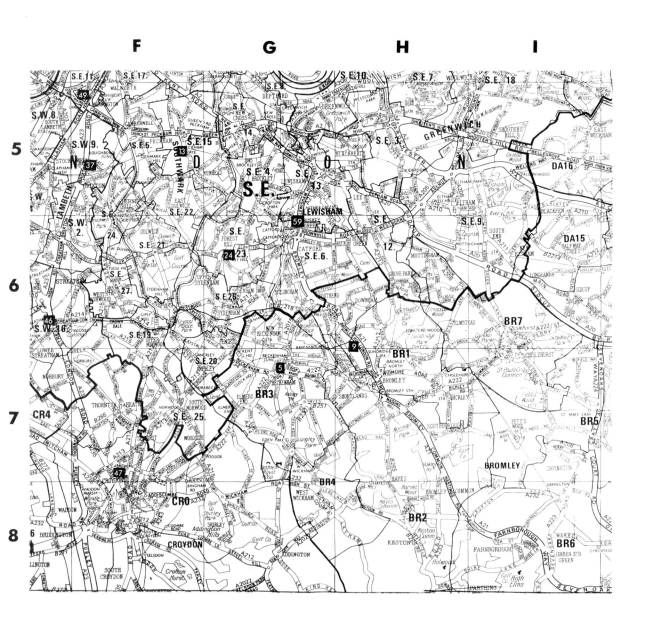

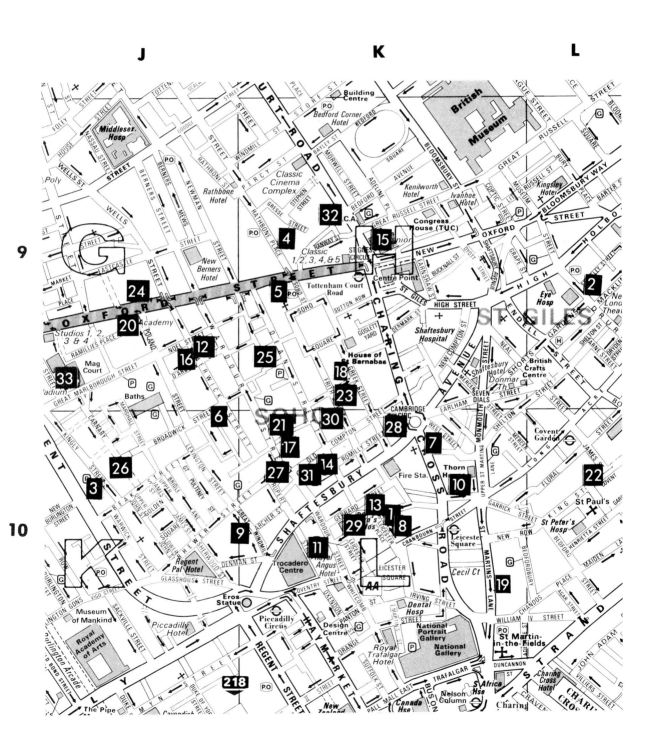

ADDRESSES

NB. Location numbers preceded by an S refer to the Soho Map; all others appear on the Greater London Map. Where a venue was used at various times by different clubs, the name of the building **is used as the main entry (usually a pub name), with** see **references from the club names. If no such overall name exists, the full entry is given for the first club using those premises to appear in the alphabetical sequence, with** see **references from the others.**

1 **ACTON TOWN HALL**
High Street
London W3
(MAP REF. C4)

S 1 **AD-LIB, The**
7 Leicester Place
London W1
(now an office block called Charles House. NB: the Ad-Lib was on an upper floor and reached by a lift. The short-lived Cavern club was in the basement)
(MAP REF. K10)

2 **ALL SAINT'S HALL**
Powis Gardens
London W11
(MAP REF. D4)

S 2 **ARTS LAB, The**
182 Drury Lane
London WC2
(ground floor premises are now owned by Philip Poole & Co., a shop specialising in calligraphic supplies)
(MAP REF. L9)

3 **ASTORIA, FINSBURY PARK**
232 Seven Sisters Road
London N4
(became famous in the 1970s as the Rainbow)
(MAP REF. F2)

4 **ATTIC, The**
1a Hounslow High Street
Hounslow
Middx.
(MAP REF. B5)

S 3 **BAG O'NAILS**
8 Kingly Street
London W1
(MAP REF. J10)

S 4 **BALLADS AND BLUES CLUB**
The Black Horse
6 Rathbone Place
London W1
(MAP REF. K9)

S 5 **BEAT CITY**
79 Oxford Street
London W1
(currently closed, about to reopen as a wine bar)
(MAP REF. K9)

5 **BECKENHAM ARTS LAB**
The Three Tuns
High Street
Beckenham
Kent
(MAP REF. G5)

6 **BLUE HORIZON CLUB**
Nag's Head
205 York Road
Battersea
London SW11
(MAP REF. E5)

BLUE OPERA CLUB
See **COOK'S FERRY INN**

BLUES AND BARRELHOUSE CLUB
See **ROUNDHOUSE**
(Soho)

A D D R E S S E S

BLUESVILLE CLUBS
See **THE MANOR HOUSE, HORNSEY WOOD TAVERN**

7 BOTTLENECK BLUES CLUB
Railway Tavern
Angel Lane
London E15
(MAP REF. G3)

8 BREADBASKET, The
65 Cleveland Street
London W1
(MAP REF. E4)

S 6 BRICKLAYER'S ARMS, The
7 Broadwick Street
London W1
(still there)
(MAP REF. J10)

9 BROMEL CLUB, The
Bromley Court Hotel
Bromley Hill
Kent
(MAP REF. H6)

10 BULL'S HEAD, The
Junction of Lonsdale Road
and Barnes High Street
Barnes, London SW13
(MAP REF. C5)

S 7 BUNJIES
27 Litchfield Street
London WC2
(still there)
(MAP REF. K10)

S 8 CAVERN, The
7 Leicester Place
London W1
(basement of Charles House, still used
for gigs, now known as Notre Dame
Hall)
(MAP REF. K10)

S 9 CLUB 11
Ham Yard
41 Great Windmill Street
London W1
(to enter this and the later clubs on the
site you passed through the street
frontage and out to the club entrance in
Ham Yard. The street frontage has now
gone and Ham Yard is mostly taken up
by a car park)
(MAP REF. K10)

11 CLUB NOREIK
834 Seven Sisters Road
London N15
(at the junction w/High Road,
Tottenham)
(MAP REF. F2)

COLISEUM
See **LONDON COLISEUM**

COLONEL BAREFOOT'S ROCK GARDEN
See **EEL PIE ISLAND**

S 10 COLYER CLUB, The
10-12 Great Newport Street
London WC2
(currently derelict)
(MAP REF. K10)

12 COOK'S FERRY INN
River Lea, Towpath off
Angel Road
London N18
(MAP REF. G1)

13 CO-OP HALL
Rye Lane
Peckenham
London SE15
(MAP REF. F5)

14 COUNTRY CLUB, The
210a Haverstock Hill
London NW3
(MAP REF. E3)

CRAWDADDY, The
See **STATION HOTEL
RICHMOND ATHLETIC ASSOC.
STAR HOTEL**

15 CROMWELLIAN, The
3 Cromwell Road
London SW7
(club still exists in the same premises)
(MAP REF. E4)

16 CROWN, The
174 Richmond Road
Twickenham
Mddx
(MAP REF. B6)

17 DERBY ARMS, The
565 Upper Richmond Road West
London SW14
(MAP REF. C5)

18 EALING CLUB, The
Helena Chambers (basement)
Broadway
Ealing
London W5
(MAP REF. B4)

19 EAST HAM GRANADA
281 Barking Road
London E6
(MAP REF. H3)

20 EEL PIE ISLAND
(The island is approached by a
footbridge at the end of Water Lane,
Twickenham, Mddx. The hotel and
dance hall were on the far side of the
island)
(MAP REF. B6)

21 **FISHMONGER'S ARMS**
287 High Road
London N22
(MAP REF. F1)

S 11 **FLAMINGO, The (also
The All Nighter, The
Whiskey A Go Go)**
33-37 Wardour Street
London W1
(The ground floor which held the
Whiskey is now the WAG club. Also
note in 1967-8, the Flamingo was
known as the Pink Flamingo)
(MAP REF. K10)

22 **FOLK BARGE, The**
Townend Wharf
Kingston-upon-Thames
(MAP REF. B7)

23 **FOX AND GOOSE HOTEL**
Hanger Lane
Ealing
London W5
(MAP REF. B3)

S 12 **FREIGHT TRAIN**
44 Berwick Street
London W1
(During the late 1960s the premises
were used by Musicland, one of the
best record shops of the era. Currently
'Fellini', a boutique)
(MAP REF. J9)

24 **GLENLYN, The**
Waldram Place
Forest Hill
London SE23
(MAP REF. G6)

25 **GOLDHAWK SOCIAL
CLUB, The**
205 Goldhawk Road
London W12
(renamed Shepherd's Bush Club, as
such still there)
(MAP REF. D4)

S 13 **GOOD EARTH**
44 Gerrard Street
London W1
(now a Chinese supermarket)
(MAP REF. K10)

GRANADA TOOTING
See **TOOTING GRANADA**

75 **HALF MOON, The**
93 Lower Richmond Road
Putney
London SW15
(MAP REF. D5)

26 **HANGING LAMP, The**
St Elizabeth's RC Church
The Vineyard
Richmond-upon-Thames
(the club was in the crypt)
(MAP REF. C5)

HAPPENING 44
See **GOOD EARTH**

S 14 **HEAVEN AND HELL**
57 Old Compton Street
London W1
(Along with the premises used by the
2Is next door, the whole street level is
now Le Bistingo — a restaurant)
(MAP REF. K10)

27 **HORNSEY WOOD TAVERN**
376 Seven Sisters Road
London N4
(MAP REF. F2)

S 15 **HORSESHOES, The**
264 Tottenham Court Road
London W1
(still there but currently derelict pending
refurbishing)
(MAP REF. K9)

S 16 **HOUSE OF SAM WIDGES**
9 D'Arblay Street
(corner of Berwick Street)
London W1
(currently a betting shop)
(MAP REF. J9)

28 **JAZZ BARGE, The**
(probably Townend Wharf,
Kingston-upon-Thames)
(MAP REF. B7)

29 **JAZZ CELLAR, The**
22a High Street
Kingston-upon-Thames
(NB: by the mid 1960s the 'jazz' part
had been dropped)
(MAP REF. B7)

30 **KAZZOO KLUB**
Wallington Public Hall
Stafford Road
Wallington
Surrey
(MAP REF. E8)

31 **KLOOK'S KLEEK**
Railway Hotel
100 West End Lane
London NW6
(The Railway has been used for music
on and off over the years)
(MAP REF. D3)

LAURIE'S, Cy
See **Club 11**

S 17 **LE MACABRE**
23 Meard Street
London W1
(most recently a restaurant, now
derelict)
(MAP REF. K10)

S 18 **LES COUSINS**
49 Greek Street
London W1
(The basement is currently used by a
club called Lucky Pierre's. The ground
floor restaurant was a Chinese
restaurant until recently but is currently
closed)
(MAP REF. K9)

A D D R E S S E S

S 19 LONDON COLISEUM
St Martin's Lane
London WC2
(MAP REF. K10)

32 MADDINGLEY, The
Willoughby Road
E. Twickenham
(NB: the building was gutted by fire in the last few years and is currently derelict)
(MAP REF. B5)

33 MANOR HOUSE, The
316 Green Lanes
London N4
(opp. Manor Hse. tube)
(MAP REF. F2)

S 20 MARQUEE, The (1958-64)
165 Oxford Street
London W1
(MAP REF. J9)

S 21 MARQUEE, The (1964-date)
90 Wardour Street
London W1
(MAP REF. K10)

S 22 MIDDLE EARTH
43 King Street
Covent Garden
London WC2
(The house, much restored, is still there. The company who use the upper floors as offices presumably also make use of the old basement)
See also **the Roundhouse (Chalk Farm)**
(MAP REF. L10)

S 23 MOKA, The
29 Frith Street
London W1
(MAP REF. K9)

34 OLDFIELD HALL
Off Oldfield Lane
Greenford,
Middx.
(MAP REF. B3)

S 24 100 CLUB
100 Oxford Street
London W1
(still there)
(MAP REF. J9)

S 25 PARTISAN, The
7 Carlisle Street
London W1
(for many years the whole building had been used by various left-wing organisations. Recently refurbished and awaiting letting)
(MAP REF. K9)

PICCADILLY JAZZ CLUB
See **Club 11**

35 PONTIAC CLUB
Zeeta House
200 Upper Richmond Road
London SW15
(MAP REF. D5)

36 RAILWAY HOTEL, The
The Bridge
Station Approach
Wealdstone
Harrow, Middx.
(MAP REF. B2)

37 RAM JAM CLUB
390 Brixton Road
London SW9
(MAP REF. F5)

38 REFECTORY, The
911 Finchley Road
London NW11
(MAP REF. D2)

39 REVOLUTION, The
14-16 Bruton Place
London W1
(currently the Burlesque Club)
(MAP REF. E4)

RICHARDSON'S REHEARSAL ROOMS
See **GOOD EARTH**

40 RICHMOND ATHLETIC ASSOC.
Twickenham Road
Richmond-upon-Thames
(The second Richmond Craw-daddy Club location. Later used for gigs after the demise of the Crawdaddy)
(MAP REF. B5)

RICKY TICK, The
See **ATTIC, The**
(NB: Although there were a number of Ricky Tick Clubs, most were too far out of London to be covered in this book. Only the one in Hounslow is covered)

S 26 ROARING 20's, The
50 Carnaby Street
London W1
(basement of what is now known as Stanley House, an office block)
(MAP REF. J10)

41 ROUNDHOUSE, The (Chalk Farm)
Chalk Farm Road
London NW1
(used regularly until the late 1970s for music)
(MAP REF. E3)

42 ROUND HOUSE, The (Dagenham)
Lodge Avenue
Dagenham
Essex
(MAP REF. I3)

S 27 ROUNDHOUSE, The (Soho)
83 Wardour Street (junction of Brewer St)
London W1
(now a strip club and pool hall)
(MAP REF. K10)

ONE HUNDRED + SEVENTY 1

A D D R E S S E S

43 ROYAL DANCE HALL, TOTTENHAM
413 High Road
London N17
(MAP REF. F2)

ROYAL FOREST HOTEL
Ranger's Road
London E4.
(Not on map)

44 RUSKIN ARMS
386 High Street North
London E12
(MAP REF. H3)

THE SCENE
See **Club 11**
(NB: In 1965 the club reopened as the New Scene)

45 SCOTCH OF ST JAMES
13 Mason's Yard
London SW1
(now 'Director's Lodge' Club)
(MAP REF. E4)

S 28 SCOT'S HOOSE
Cambridge Circus
London W1
(currently the Spice of Life Disco)
(MAP REF. K10)

S 29 SCOTT's, Ronnie (Old Place)
39 Gerrard Street
London W1
(for many years the premises have been used as offices)
(MAP REF. K10)

S 30 SCOTT's, Ronnie
47 Frith Street
London W1
(still there)
(MAP REF. K10)

46 SILVER BLADES ICE RINK
386 Streatham High Road
London SW16
(MAP REF. E6)

SKIFFLE CELLAR
See **LES COUSINS**

47 STAR HOTEL
296 London Road
Broad Green
Croydon, Surrey
(This was part of the Crawdaddy circuit. Later in the 1960s gigs were held there but without a club name)
(MAP REF. F7)

48 STATION HOTEL, The
1 Kew Road
Richmond-upon-Thames
(the first Crawdaddy location)
(MAP REF. B5)

STUDIO 51
See **COLYER CLUB**

49 SURREY ROOMS
The Oval
Kennington
London SE11
(MAP REF. F5)

50 TAGG'S ISLAND
Hampton Court Road
Hampton, Mddx.
(in the Thames between Hampton and Hampton Court)
(MAP REF. B7)

TEMPLE, The
See **FLAMINGO, The**

51 THAMES HOTEL, The
Hampton Court Way
East Molesey, Surrey
(on the south side of Hampton Court Bridge)
(MAP REF. B7)

TILES
See **BEAT CITY**

52 TOBY JUG, The
1 Hook Rise
Tolworth, Surrey
(MAP REF. C8)

53 TOOTING GRANADA
50 Mitcham Road
Tooting
London SW17
(MAP REF. E6)

TOTTENHAM ROYAL
See **ROYAL DANCE HALL**

54 TROUBADOUR COFFEE HOUSE, The
265 Old Brompton Road
London SW5
(still there and looking much the same)
(MAP REF. D5)

S 31 2Is
59 Old Compton Street
London W1
(see 'Heaven & Hell')
(MAP REF. K10)

S 32 UFO
31 Tottenham Court Road
London W1
(the whole stretch of Tottenham Crt. Rd of which UFO was part, was pulled down and replaced with shops/office development. The old UFO basement has probably been filled in)
See also, **The Roundhouse (Chalk Farm)**
(MAP REF. K9)

55 UPPER CUT CLUB
Woodgrange Road
Forest Gate
London E7
(currently a bingo and social club)
(MAP REF. H3)

56 WEATHERBY ARMS, The
500 King's Road
London SW10
(MAP REF. E5)

57 **WHITE HART, The**
264 High Street
Acton
London W3
(MAP REF. C4)

58 **WHITE HART, The
(Southall)**
49 High Street
Southall, Middx
(MAP REF. A4)

59 **WITCHDOCTOR, The**
Rushey Green
Catford
London SE6
(MAP REF. G6)

WYKEHAM HALL
Market Place
Romford
Essex
(Not on map)

ZAMBESI, The
See **The Attic**

Other places of interest mentioned in the book.

60 **ABBEY ROAD CROSSING**
Abbey Road
London NW8
(by the junction of Abbey Road and
Grove End Road)
(MAP REF. D3)

61 **ALEXANDRA PALACE**
London N22
(MAP REF. E2)

62 **APPLE BOUTIQUE**
94 Baker Street
London W1
(MAP REF. E4)

63 **APPLE OFFICES**
95 Wigmore Street
London W1
(MAP REF. E4)

64 **APPLE OFFICES**
3 Savile Row
London W1
(MAP REF. E4)

65 **APPLE OFFICES**
29 St James's Street
London SW1
(MAP REF. E4)

66 **BBC TELEVISION THEATRE**
Shepherd's Bush Green
London W12
(MAP REF. D4)

67 **DECCA STUDIOS**
165 Broadhurst Gdns
London NW6
(MAP REF. D3)

68 **EMI STUDIOS, ABBEY ROAD**
3 Abbey Road
London NW8
(MAP REF. D3)

69 **EMPIRE POOL, WEMBLEY
(now WEMBLEY ARENA)**
Empire Way
Wembley
Middx.
(MAP REF. C3)

70 **HAMMERSMITH ODEON**
Queen Caroline Street
London W6
(MAP REF. D4)

71 **GEORGE HARRISON AND
RINGO STARR'S FIRST
LONDON FLAT**
Whaddon House
William Mews
London SW1
(MAP REF. E4)

72 **JOHN LENNON'S FIRST
LONDON FLAT**
13 Emperor's Gate
London SW1
(MAP REF. D4)

S 33 **LONDON PALLADIUM**
8 Argyle Street
London W1
(MAP REF. J9)

73 **REDIFFUSION STUDIOS**
Empire Way
Wembley
Middx.
(MAP REF. C3)

74 **ROYAL ALBERT HALL**
Kensington Gore
London SW7
(MAP REF. E4)

FURTHER READING

Bacon, David and Maslov, N., The Beatles' England **(Columbus Books, 1982)**

Barnes, Richard, The Who: Maximum R & B **(Eel Pie, 1982)**

Carr, Roy, The Rolling Stones: An Illustrated Record **(New English Library, 1976)**

Grime, Kitty, Jazz At Ronnie Scott's **(Robert Hale, 1979)**

Hewison, Robert, Under Siege: Literary Life In London, 1939–45 **(Weidenfeld & Nicholson, 1977)**

Humphries, Patrick, Meet On The Ledge: A History of Fairport Convention **(Eel Pie, 1982)**

—— Bookends: The Simon & Garfunkel Story **(Proteus, 1982)**

Melly, George, Owning Up **(Weidenfeld & Nicholson, 1965)**

Miles, David Bowie Black Book **(Omnibus Press, 1980)**

Norman, Philip, Shout: The True Story Of The Beatles **(Hamish Hamilton, 1981)**

—— The Stones **(Elm Tree Books, 1984)**

Nuttall, Jeff, Bomb Culture **(MacGibbon & Kee, 1968)**

Platt, John, Dreja, C and McCarty, J. Yardbirds **(Sidgwick & Jackson, 1983)**

Rawlings, Terry, Small Faces: All Our Yesterdays **(Riot Stories, 1982)**

Savage, Jon, The Kinks: The Official Biography **(Faber & Faber, 1984)**

INDEX

I N D E X